"Lord,

Help Me *NOT*
to Have These

Evil

Thoughts!"

*A practical, scriptural guide to achieving a healthy
thought-life while engaged in mental welfare.*

by **Harold Vaughan**

Christ Life Publications
P.O. Box 399
Vinton, VA 24179

Copyright © 1988, 1994 by Christ Life Publications

Third Printing

Printed in the United States of America

ISBN: 0-942889-04-5

Table of Contents

Chapter 1   Rethinking Temptation 1

Chapter 2   Recognizing the Source 10

Chapter 3   Reevaluating the Conflict 18

Chapter 4   Renunciation of the Past 22

Chapter 5   Reconciliation Where Needed 30

Chapter 6   Reckoning on Christ's Authority 37

Chapter 7   Resist the Enemy 46

Chapter 8   Rejoice in Temptation 49

Chapter 9   Rhythm and the Thought Life 54

Chapter 10   Renewing the Mind 58

Chapter 11   Robed for Battle 61

Chapter 12   Reigning with Him 72

Introduction

Satan is waging war against the minds of believers. While we cannot "look for the Devil under every rock," for preoccupation with the Devil is neither healthy nor helpful, we cannot treat the enemy of our souls too lightly. In conservative circles, there has been too little practical teaching on how satanic forces influence our minds, and too little emphasis on the scriptural procedures to liberate the thought-life.

May the Lord use this book to free many from plaguing evil thoughts.

— Harold Vaughan

Chapter 1

Rethinking Temptation

The fall night is pleasant, and you go to sleep with the windows open. Initially, a thin bedsheet provides adequate covering. The temperature gradually drops, and around 2 a.m. you are half asleep and shivering, but too drowsy to get up and get a blanket out of the closet. If you are married you wish your mate would wake up and get more cover. You are cold enough to be miserable, but not awake enough to do anything about it! Your lack of initiative makes the whole night a chilly, half-conscious experience that you will regret the next day.

Temptation is much the same. As believers we do not want to yield, yet, as humans, we have impulses that crave fulfillment.

The True Basis of Temptation

"If I were really spiritual, really close to God, I would not have all these vile thoughts and lurid temptations." Many of us have readily accepted the notion that temptation is the result of our sinfulness. But wait a minute! Jesus was tempted. Was He sinful? No! Eve was tempted in her unfallen state. She was not sinful when she encountered the beguiling serpent. Today we must also contend with the flesh (fallen nature), but temptation took place prior to the Fall.

Someone said, "Temptation is an enticement to fulfill a God-given drive in a God-forbidden way." This is the true basis of temptation. *"But every man is tempted, when he is drawn away of his own lust* [desires] *and enticed" (James 1:14).* Temptation allures us to fulfill a legitimate desire in an illegitimate way.

In order to understand temptation we must understand life. What actually took place when God breathed the "breath of life" into man? Life is a force that consists of drives or desires. Imagine what life was like prior to the Fall. In the pristine state, everything God made was flawless. God made man and gave him certain appetites. Adam had pure desires for creativity, sexual fulfillment, worship, fellowship, food, work, approval, justice, beauty, knowledge, and holiness. God gave man a way to express and satisfy these needs.

Man's God-Given Drives

Dominion. Man was made to have dominion in his world. God created Adam and put him into the Garden of Eden to dress it and to keep it (Gen. 2:15). Adam was instructed to *"replenish the earth, and subdue it: and have dominion...over every living thing" (Gen. 1:28).* God intended that man occupy the highest place among the creatures of earth and exercise his ruling privilege over them. Prior to the Fall, the drive to rule was unperverted.

Hunger. When God designed the human body, He gave man a desire for food. The Garden of Eden had an abundance of delicious fruit to satisfy this need.

Sexuality. The sex drive was God's idea. By His design a man and woman desire a relationship unique to humankind, for no other creature combines this desire with love. This is "good," like everything else God made, and becomes wrong only when used outside the intended bounds. With every desire the Lord gave man, He also made a way to satisfy and express it. Sex is not evil, but the distortion and prohibitory use of sex produces evil.

Supernatural. Earth bound man was created to have supernatural fellowship with Holy God. Divine communion was the privilege and portion allotted to Adam and Eve. Though bound by a physical body man was created in the image of God. That means Adam possessed mind, will, and emotions in moral likeness to God. This desire and capacity for fellowship with God lifted man out of the plane of mere earthly existence.

Creativity. God made man to express creativity. When called upon to name the animals, Adam's creativity drive assisted him. There are thousands of ways to express creativity — music, or art, or engineering, or decorating, or writing, are only a few. Creative people are exciting to be around. We never know what they are going to do next! This drive reflects the image of the Creator, and prior to sin was an aid to man.

Beauty. Man, with a built-in love for the aesthetic, is naturally attracted to beautiful things. Why else would people travel across the world to look at paintings, or architecture, or to take photographs of nature? Man has an innate desire for beauty.

Worship. Man was created to worship. Adam enjoyed God and loved to worship. All this changed when sin came into the picture. When a person comes to Christ, the desire to worship is reactivated.

Justice. God is just, and His creation has a desire for justice. God never intended for man to ignore those who mistreat him. He demands justice, but in his fallen state, man confuses justice with revenge! Man cannot be neutral when treated wrongly. That only leads to resentment. The human response is to take revenge, but the biblical method for taking revenge is to, *"Do good to them that hate you" (Matt. 5:44).* God will balance the scales one day, but in the meantime, we need to do good to those who take advantage of us. How is your justice drive functioning?

Approval. Healthy people need approval. Anyone who would say, "I don't care what anybody thinks" needs help. Just as a loving child wants acceptance and approval from his parents, the child of God longs for approval from his heavenly Father. At the baptism of Jesus, God gave verbal approval to His Son, even though the Lord Jesus had not yet preached a sermon, won a soul, cast out a devil, or done a miracle. He had not even begun His public ministry. Nevertheless, His Father showered approval on Him. *"Thou art my beloved Son; in thee I am well pleased" (Luke 3:22).*

Jesus loved to hear His Father's words of approval! His acceptance was not the result of production; it was the result of His position!

Do you want to be approved by God? The Father loves to have His children in a position where He can express His approval of us. God showed His pleasure with Job when He bragged about him to the Devil. *"Hast thou considered my servant Job, that there is none like him in the earth?" (Job 1:8).* When we are totally submitted to God, He delights in us. Desire for approval is normal as long as we seek it in proper order — God first and man second.

Fellowship. *"It is not good that the man should be alone" (Gen. 2:18).* Man was designed for fellowship. Interaction and interdependence are the biblical norm. Isolation from others was not God's original plan.

A Symphony

These and other drives were all in Adam, an orchestrated symphony, cooperating to produce a beautiful masterpiece. In the original state there was no conflict, no disunity. Each desire functioned in its proper place, and all were wholesome and good in and of themselves.

Temptation Illustrated

The serpent (Satan) came along, established contact, and tempted Eve to sin.

> *Now the serpent was more subtil than any beast of the field which the Lord God had made. And he said unto the woman, Yea, hath God said, Ye shall not eat of every tree of the garden?*
>
> *And the woman said unto the serpent, We may eat of the fruit of the trees of the garden:*
>
> *But of the fruit of the tree which is in the midst of the garden, God hath said, Ye shall not eat of it, neither shall ye touch it, lest ye die.*
>
> *And the serpent said unto the woman, ye shall not surely die:*
>
> *For God doth know that in the day ye eat*

*thereof, then your eyes shall be opened, and ye
shall be as gods, knowing good and evil.*

*And when the woman saw that the tree was
good for food, and that it was pleasant to the eyes,
and a tree to be desired to make one wise, she took
of the fruit thereof, and did eat, and gave also unto
her husband with her; and he did eat (Gen. 3:1-6).*

Satan maligned God's character in verse 1 and accused God of
lying in verse 4. Then came the temptation. In verse 5 he appealed
to Eve's supernatural drive by telling her, *"Ye shall be as gods,
knowing good and evil."* Here Satan is appealing to Eve's capacity
for pride. She is innocent in regard to evil. It was God's desire she
never know evil. Satan entices her with the prospect of becoming
as a "god." He aroused her hunger drive *"when the woman saw that
the tree was good for food."* Notice how our drives follow us
around. They go wherever we go. Hunger accompanied Eve this
day, and the Devil took advantage of it. The next avenue of
enticement played upon the aesthetic drive. *"It was pleasant to
look upon."* Then Satan told Eve it was *"a tree to be desired to
make one wise."* He stimulated Eve's desire for knowledge.

Eve committed no sin up to this point. She was merely enticed
to fulfill God-given drives in God-forbidden ways. She should
have said no to the Devil's allurement. Unhappily, she yielded to
the enticement and disobeyed God. Sin is transgression of God's
law in utilizing our capabilities in an illegitimate manner. Eve had
no idea of the consequences of her sin.

Satan used the same approach on Jesus. He sought to get Jesus
to illegitimately satisfy legitimate desires, by appealing to three
drives.

*Then was Jesus led up of the Spirit into the
wilderness to be tempted of the devil. And when he
had fasted forty days and forty nights, he was
afterward an hungred. And when the tempter came
to him, he said, If thou be the Son of God, command*

that these stones be made bread. But he answered and said, It is written, Man shall not live by bread alone, but by every word that proceedeth out of the mouth of God (Matt. 4:1-4).

Interestingly, he prefaced the enticement with, *"If thou be the Son of God,"* as if Christ had to prove anything to Satan! Jesus had been without food for 40 days. He was hungry. *"Command that these stones be made bread."* Jesus was the Son of God, and He could have turned those stones into bread, but that was not God's will. Therefore Jesus refused to satisfy a legitimate need in this way. Christ would not be intimidated to prove Satan's point. Neither do we have to be intimidated or establish a point of agreement with the Devil.

Second, *"... the devil taketh him up into the holy city, and setteth him on a pinnacle of the temple....If thou be the Son of God, cast thyself down: for it is written, He shall give his angels charge concerning thee: and in their hands they shall bear thee up, lest at any time thou dash thy foot against a stone" (Matt.4:56).* He sought to get Jesus in another defensive dilemma. *"If...."* This verse shows how Satan is a Bible scholar. He can even (mis)quote Scripture if he deems it necessary. To which drive did Satan appeal? "Jump off the building and let God take care of it." Prior to the incarnation the Son had all the power and ability of the transcendent God. However, He chose to humble Himself and limit His power temporarily. He was subject to the natural laws He had established. Therefore, Satan appealed to the Divine when he enticed Him to disregard the law of gravity. Prior to the incarnation He was not bound by this law. Only something supernatural could override this law. Appealing directly to Omnipotence, Satan tried to get Jesus to use God's power for his own ends. Had He been successful in persuading Jesus to leap off, he would have gotten Him to act foolishly in presuming on His Father.

"Again, the devil...sheweth him all the kingdoms of the world...And saith unto him, All these things will I give thee, if thou

wilt fall down and worship me" (Matt. 4:8-9). Here Satan played upon the legitimate desire to reign. Jesus will in fact rule the kingdoms of the earth, ultimately establishing His throne in righteousness during the millennial reign. But the adversary tempted Him to fulfill the desire to rule before the prescribed time, and by sinful means Satan wanted Jesus to worship him! The real goal of Satan is to divert to himself the worship due to God. Satan commonly tempts us to use the wrong means at the wrong time to achieve a legitimate goal. Jesus will rule the earth, but not until the appropriate time, and He will never bow to Satan for any reason!

Sin's Effect on the Drives

As we have seen, temptation is the enticement to fulfill legitimate desires by illegitimate means. When Eve yielded to temptation, *"lust conceived and brought forth sin."* Had Eve known what was in store for her and the human race, surely she would not have done it. The damage was done. God had given stern warning, *"In the day that thou eatest thereof thou shalt surely die."* The sentence of death was in effect. Man had become a sinner, with all the devastating consequences. Sin always destroys and distorts. Ever since the Fall man has been abnormal. Many people today are at war within themselves. Their drives pull them apart because sin has warped the appetites of man.

In some people, the drives that were intended to be refined and beautiful have become exaggerated, ugly monsters. The sex drive has become an overbearing master to many, occupying too large a place and demanding to be fed constantly. Our society seems to overindulge in sensuality. In its place, sexual fulfillment is beautiful; out of place it becomes tainted and sordid.

In some cases the sex drive is perverted toward what the Bible calls "vile affections," or an unnatural attraction between members of the same sex. (This area could be the subject for an entire volume.)

On the other hand, sin has caused some to feel that sex is evil within itself. This is obviously erroneous. God declared that all He made was "good." The misuse and misunderstanding of sexual appetites and gratification cause untold heartache. God provided a valid means of satisfying every desire He created. Sexual expression finds its legitimate fulfillment within the framework of marriage.

Look how the hunger drive has been perverted. Interestingly, Satan appealed to this drive in the garden with Eve and on the mountain with Jesus. Eating disorders are epidemic. Some are starving themselves while others are gorging themselves. We live in a nation where overeating is accepted. The Scripture refers to gluttony as sin. Some cannot control this drive.

The drive to succeed is easily distorted. God wants us to have a healthy desire to achieve in life, but not by dominating others and trampling them in the process. Today, success is equated with money, fame, and power, but true success is becoming what God wants us to be.

Sin's effect on some drives has made them weak when they should be strong and vibrant. The drive to rule or have dominion should be strong and healthy. Most people today cannot rule their own lives, much less their households. Lack of self-control abounds. A person comes to the altar and makes a decision, but he is unable to follow through. Why? His rule drive is weak and the other drives overshadow it. He wants to do the right thing, but conflicting desires make him incapable of performing. Conversely, the desire to rule dominates some people, who, like Hitler, become tyrants. But in most cases man has lost his quest for dominion.

Modern man's desire for creativity is greatly diminished. Imitation is easier than initiation, so most people operate like drones, doing only what they must to get by. Creativity is a distinguishing feature of humanity. Through it man reflects God — the Creator of all things. We should not be surprised that sin damaged creativity to this extent.

Other drives were short-circuited when man sinned. Man's natural desire to worship the one true God was misdirected after the Fall. Today he can be found worshiping the sun, stone idols, nature, or even himself as the secular humanists promote man as the measure and end of all things.

Moderation

Man's drives are like piano strings. When a piano gets out of tune, a tuner adjusts the strings. Some strings need to be loosened, others tightened. The tuner works until each string plays on pitch. God has given us the Holy Spirit to moderate our drives. Some drives need to be toned down. Others need to be revitalized. Do you possess any overbearing drives, any weak drives that need adjustment? The Lord will not remove drives, but He will tune them. Remember, in the Garden of Eden man's drives were like a symphony. They were in cohesion, not conflict.

Tune-ups can be painful, but the beautiful music is worth it! Just as instruments need periodic adjustment, so man also needs regular maintenance. Invite Jesus Christ into your heart to be your Lord. Then cooperate with His Holy Spirit while He moderates your drives. You will never be what God desires until you allow His Holy Spirit to do His adjusting work.

Weather conditions, temperature, and location all have a bearing on a piano's performance and sound quality. Likewise, many things influence our drives. This is why the Bible says, *"Count it all joy when you fall into various temptations."* Temptation presents an opportunity for growth in Christ likeness and patience (James 1:3). Through temptation God makes us aware of the functioning order of our drives. When we are tempted, we should REJOICE! God is working in us the ongoing process of sanctification. He uses temptation to show areas where we need moderation, either an increase or decrease in intensity. Rely on Christ as your Lord (Master). Respond daily to the promptings of the Spirit and experience the beautiful music!

Chapter 2

Recognizing the Source

We will live defeated lives if we do not recognize the nature of the Adversary and the type of conflict in which we are engaged. Satan has so effectively camouflaged himself that we often do not even remember that he exists. Most believers have no practical theology on combating Satan. Some feel that Satan and demons exist only among the heathen tribes on the mission field, if at all, and certainly not here in civilized America! Another false notion is that if we talk about the Devil he might show up! This prevailing ignorance obviously exposes Satan's strategy to blind us to the extent of his work. There must be an unseen conspiracy behind this veil of darkness. *"Be sober, be vigilant; because your adversary the devil...walketh about, seeking whom he may devour"* (I Peter 5:8). Scripture tells us to be alert, not to hide our heads in the sand. The "ostrich syndrome" has brought about a condition where the present-day church offers very little threat to the Devil.

Two Sources

"Doth a fountain send forth at the same place sweet water and bitter?" (James 3:11). Two basic sources operate in the cosmos. God is the fountainhead of all that is good and holy. Satan is the ultimate source of sin and corruption. All thoughts, philosophies, and attitudes can eventually be traced to one of these two sources.

The Power of Suggestion

The power of influence cannot be overestimated. Ideas and concepts are mighty weapons, influencing the destinies of nations.

Ideas give birth to explosive consequences. Consider how Adolph Hitler captured the imagination of the German people. The tools of communication he utilized were minimal in comparison with the sources of manipulation available in our modern media.

Thousands of thoughts come to our mind every day without our volition. Where do all these thoughts come from? Many believers are frustrated with themselves for having wicked thoughts. The Holy Spirit can bring things to our remembrance, but satanic forces also influence our thinking. If we do not, by an act of our own will, stir up these evil thoughts, the wicked imaginations parading across our minds are not ours. They are inserted by Satan. The undiscerning, yet sincere, believer may blame himself for the host of unwholesome thoughts.

Scripture clearly tells us that God does not tempt us with evil (James 1:13). God is not the source. You may say, "The flesh is to blame. It must be the carnal nature acting up." Wicked impulses could very well come from the flesh (old nature). However, the Lord dealt with the evil nature at His Cross. *"They that are Christ's have crucified the flesh with the affections and lusts" (Gal 5:24).* This inner crucifixion is a matter of faith in what God has said.

When we have agreed with God and reckoned ourselves dead to sin and alive to God, why do we still have problems with the thought-life? The source of the believer's conflict is from anti-God forces at work in the world in which we live. Having had thousands of years to study humanity, the evil forces know exactly how to introduce their streams into our thinking with expert timing.

Thought Implantation

In Matthew 16:22-23 Jesus begins to tell His disciples of His suffering, death, and resurrection. *"Then Peter took him, and began to rebuke him...But he [Jesus] turned, and said unto Peter, Get thee behind me, Satan: thou art an offence unto me."* Jesus was not talking to Peter, but to the one controlling Peter! Obviously Peter had accepted and entertained thoughts from Satan, and he was being used as Satan's mouthpiece. His verbalizing of these satanic suggestions brought a stern rebuke from our Lord. It is not a light matter to cooperate with Satan in manifesting his thoughts and actions!

Satanic forces begin their war on the saints by attacking our thinking apparatus. No wonder God gave us the helmet of salvation and the shield of faith to quench the fiery thought-darts of Satan. The battle for the mind is so fierce that God has given us ample information and weaponry to bring "into captivity every thought to the obedience of Christ."

Ananias and Sapphira are examples of Satan's mind tactics. They sold some property and gave the impression that they had contributed all the money to the church, but they had pocketed part of the proceeds. *"But Peter said, Ananias, why hath Satan filled thine heart to lie to the Holy Ghost?" (Acts 5:3).* Peter referred to this desire to establish a reputation as satanic. Satan introduced the proposal and Ananias accepted it. The implanted idea soon found outward expression in a lie, an expression of the Devil. Jesus called Satan *"a liar, and the father of it" (John 8:44).* Every lie ever told signifies cooperation with the original liar — he is a deceiver!

Scripture gives no reason to believe that Ananias and Sapphira were not Christians. Christians can accept Satan's thoughts, speak Satan's words, and express Satan's actions. Remember, Satan filled Ananias' heart to lie!

Your Adversary the Devil

The Old Testament assumes the existence of Satan as much as it does the existence of God, though it offers no formal proof of either. Satan's existence is recognized by every writer of the New Testament. Nineteen of the 27 books refer to Satan by mentioning one of his names. Of the eight books that do not mention him, four imply his existence by referring to demons. The four gospels contain 29 references to Satan, 25 of which are made by Christ.

Nature of Satan

Satan is a person. He is not a principle or an influence or a figment of imagination. He possesses intellect, will, and emotion.

Satan is a creature. He is not self-existent. *"Thou wast perfect in thy ways from the day thou was created, till iniquity was found in thee" (Ezek. 28:15).* As a created being, he was infinitely less than God (see Col. 1:16).

Satan is a spirit being — finite, invisible, and immaterial. He can temporarily manifest himself visibly.

Scripture speaks of him as an "anointed cherub," seemingly the highest classification of angelic beings. Some commentators think the title "covering cherub" indicates that prior to his fall Satan was first in rank of all creatures. "Covering cherub" also indicates he was a highly stationed official for God.

Names and Titles of Satan

The names and titles given to Satan aptly describe his character. For example:

Tempter. The word *tempter* is ascribed to Satan twice in the New Testament (Matt. 4:3; 1 Thess. 3:5).

The verb to *tempt* has two senses in Scripture. One simply means "to test" as in refining gold, the process of separating the gold from the dross. Used to denote the tests and trials sent from God, this term should be interpreted in a positive sense.

The other meaning of the verb to *tempt* means "to incite to evil." This includes the idea of finding and exploiting a weak spot. When the term is applied to Satan, the objective is always negative or evil. He has no greater desire than to tempt and incite to sin. Apparently this is what he did to those celestial spirits who are called "his angels," because they *"kept not their first estate."* The cleverness of the Devil is to make himself invisible in our temptations.

Devil. *Devil* means "slanderer" or "separator." This portrays Satan as a malignant accuser. The word *devil,* derived from the Greek word *diabolos,* is used 35 times in the New Testament. In Eden Satan slandered God to Eve by casting doubt on His integrity. He also slandered Job to God by alleging Job's loyalty to be selfish in essence. Satan is never more pleased than when he can influence one Christian to slander another.

Satan. *Satan* means "adversary" or "opposer." Scripture clearly teaches he is the implacable enemy of God and man. Paul stated, *"Wherefore we would have come unto you, even I Paul, once and again; but Satan hindered us" (1 Thess. 2:18).*

Murderer. Jesus bestowed this title on Satan. *"Ye are of your father the devil....He was a murderer from the beginning, and abode not in the truth"(John 8:44).* From the dawn of history Satan has demonstrated a passion to kill and destroy. His hand was shown in the first family, where the first murder was perpetrated. Note the connection between Satan and murder in this verse, *"Not as Cain, who was of that wicked one, and slew his brother" (1 John 3:12).* Murder came naturally for Cain because he was *"of that wicked one."* Another way to put this verse is *Cain who belonged to the devil and murdered.* Actual murder is only one manifestation of Satan as murderer. Jesus went to great lengths to show that the attitude of hate is the same as committing murder in our hearts. Interestingly, the average child will witness 18,000 murders via television by the time he reaches age 16. Satan is not only the "prince of the power of the air" but also of the air waves!

Inclinations to hold grudges and harbor animosity are not from the new nature. Observe the inability of the human race to coexist peacefully. Satan is a divider and will use any means to sow strife and discord.

The rampant upsurge of self-destruction is further evidence of Satan as murderer. Teenage and child suicide are accelerating at an alarming rate. When dire circumstances and destructive spiritual forces combine, death is often the outcome. Dungeons and Dragons®, an occultic fantasy game, has been linked with many teenage suicides. Satan is a murderer!

Liar. Satan seldom tells a complete lie. Normally he mixes truth and error so the lie is not easily detected. He even quotes Scripture, but he always twists it to some degree. Satan is the fountain of all falsehood and deceit. Scripture warns that in the last days the mixture of error with truth will be so skillfully contrived that were it possible it would deceive the very elect (Matt. 24:24). *"He is a liar, and the father of it" (John 8:44).* Exaggeration and deception are expressions of his character.

The Bible warns us about "vain philosophy" and "doctrines of demons." I fear much so-called secular humanism has infiltrated the minds of believers. Deception and "empty philosophy" are a favorite "wile" of Satan. Those who are not solidly grounded in the Word of Truth are easy prey. The if-it-works-do-it mentality is quite popular today, but liberal methods are the forerunner of a diluted message. Devastating results are now being reaped from a secularized version of Christianity.

Accuser. Satan accuses God before man, as in the case of Eve. He accuses man before God, as in the case of Job. He also accuses people before each other, prompting us to judge one another. Furthermore, he accuses us before ourselves. He launches accusations, whether false or true, to rob us of peace, mar our service, and give us a sense of condemnation.

In her book *War on the Saints,* Jessie Penn Lewis writes, "Temptation is an effort to cause the man to transgress the law; accusation is an effort to place the believer in the guilty position of having transgressed the law."

Accusation can be a counterfeit for conviction. If the Enemy can get us bound up with sin-consciousness, we become spiritually paralyzed. True conviction comes from God when sin is committed. It must be confessed immediately. The believer should accept forgiveness by thanking God for cleansing. Once confessed, God will never remind the believer of his sin. If the incident comes to mind again, it is not God convicting, but Satan trying to condemn! Feelings of guilt must be refused and displaced by thanks and praise.

When the Accuser confronted Martin Luther with a list of his sins, Luther admitted to them. But then he turned to the Accuser and said, "Now write across them all," *"the blood of Jesus Christ*

His Son cleanseth us from all sin" (1 John 1:7). We must learn to use the Sword as Luther did — to put the Devil to flight!

Evil One. The Devil is the embodiment of all that is evil and unholy. For the Scripture says, *"The whole world lieth in wickedness" (1 John 5:19).*

God of This World. *"In whom the god of this world hath blinded the minds of them which believe not" (2 Cor. 4:4).* The clear implication is that Satan heads up the godless world system. He is behind the present movement to exclude God from public life. He uses self-centeredness, greed, atheistic philosophy, violence, and countless other tactics to blind men to the truth.

Angel of Light. Satan robes himself deceptively, accommodating himself to each situation. *"For Satan himself is transformed into an angel of light" (2 Cor. 11:14).* He can be sophisticated and religious. Perhaps no mask is more effective than the religious one. Obviously the whole idea of questioning biblical authority is the work of the Angel of Light!

Roaring Lion. *"Be vigilant; because your adversary the devil, as a roaring lion, walketh about, seeking whom he may devour" (1 Peter 5:8).* Just like a stalking lion, Satan's purpose is always destructive. This verse sounds a loud warning to be on the alert!

Attacker. The enemy attacks believers. An attack is not a solicitation, but an onslaught on the person's life, character, or circumstances. Satan attacked Christ when certain villagers rose up and sought to hurl Christ down a hillside (Luke 4:29); when His family charged Him with insanity (Mark 3:21); and when His enemies charged Him with demon possession (Matt. 12:24). Peter warns us of a "roaring lion" looking for opportunity to attack.

Hinderer. *"We would have come unto you...but Satan hindered us" (1 Thess. 2:18).* Paul was able to discern between the hindering of Satan and the restraining of the Spirit of God. The obstacles he places in our paths look natural and providential. We need keen discernment to distinguish them. Not all obstructions in life and ministry are ploys of Satan. However, Paul gave us ample reason to believe that Satan is indeed a hinderer.

Skeptic. The Adversary began his dealings with Eve by casting doubt on God's Word, "Hath God said?" Then he attacked God's character by accusing Him of lying. "Ye shall not surely die." The all-out attack on the credibility of the Bible has its origin in Satan, the skeptic. His skepticism has been adopted by whole denominations which disregard the Word of God. Some of the most brilliant minds are full of doubt and unbelief regarding the authority of the Bible. The church, which claims to represent the Lord, is in some cases one of God's most vocal enemies! The New Testament warned us that scoffers would appear in the last days, *"deceiving, and being deceived" (2 Tim. 3:13).* These are the ones who *"depart from the faith, giving heed to seducing spirits and doctrines of devils* [demons]*" (1 Tim. 4:1).*

Satan inserts doubt about God and His Word in the minds of serious saints. Plaguing doubts about the existence of God should be recognized for what they are — the Skeptic, maligning the character of God! *"Whatsoever is not of faith is sin" (Rom. 14:23).*

Satan has many masks. At times he works behind the scenes, so as not to be recognized. On other occasions he disguises himself in seemingly benevolent causes or in kind personalities. *"And no marvel; for Satan himself is transformed into an angel of light. Therefore it is no great thing if his ministers also be transformed as the ministers of righteousness" (2 Cor. 11:14-15).*

In summary, the conflict is on the spiritual plane. It involves unseen spirits of evil working to foil the plan of God. The Lord has given us ample knowledge, power, and weaponry to defeat the Enemy.

Chapter 3

Reevaluating the Conflict

For we wrestle not against flesh and blood, but against principalities, against powers, against the rulers of the darkness of this world, against spiritual wickedness in high places (Eph. 6:12).

There is more to life than meets the eye! There exists an invisible reality behind the physical universe. The Bible plainly tells us, *"We do not wrestle against flesh and blood."* The problem in the world today is not with people, as such, but with the nontangible entities influencing and controlling world affairs. Believers are engaged in a struggle against spiritual foes.

Ephesians tells us Satan has a hierarchy of evil. "Principalities" may refer to the highest ranking officers under Satan. The "powers" may refer to officials of somewhat lesser rank. The "rulers of darkness of this age" could be a reference to a band of wicked spirits who concentrate their efforts on human government. The "prince of Persia" held up God's messenger en route to Daniel with God's message. In fact, only Michael's assistance freed the messenger to go to Daniel. This "prince of Persia," from all indication, reigned as a powerful atmospheric spirit assigned to the country of Persia (Daniel 10). The "spiritual hosts of wickedness" may refer to hordes of unclean spirits directly above the earth.

Wherein in time past ye walked according to the course of this world, according to the prince of the power of the air, the spirit that now worketh in the children of disobedience" (Eph. 2:2). According to "this world," the "prince...of the air," and "the spirit" — notice the relationship represented here between "world," "prince," and "the spirit." Satan is referred to as the "god of this world" (2 Cor. 4:4). Satan and his evil forces dominate the entire world system. The world system does not refer to the physical universe, but of an invisible evil empire ruled by Satan.

The Unholy Spirit

Ephesians 2:2 mentioned *"the spirit that now worketh."* An *unholy spirit* dominates the lives of lost men. *"The* [unholy] *spirit that now worketh in the children of disobedience"* also seeks to work on the children of God. The Bible warns us about the *"spirit of error" (1 John 4:6)* and to *"believe not every spirit" (1 John 4:1).* The unholy spirit seeks to gain control of our minds. That is why Scripture tells us to *"be filled with the* [Holy] *Spirit" (Eph. 5:18).* Only through the continued filling of the Holy Spirit will we be able to stand against the opposing unholy spirit at work in our world.

Satan's Domain

A close reading of the Bible reveals that the satanic forces abide in the heavenlies or *"high places"* (Eph. 6:12). To our best knowledge, this "air" is located somewhere between earth and heaven, perhaps the lower atmosphere directly above the earth.

Satan is not limited in his travels. He has *access* to heaven. *"Now there was a day when the sons of God came to present themselves before the Lord, and Satan came also among them" (Job 1:6).* Further proof of Satan's access to God is found in Revelation 12:10: *"The accuser of our brethren is cast down, which accused them before our God day and night."*

In addition to *abiding* in the heavenlies and having access to heaven, Satan also is *active* on earth. *"And the Lord said unto Satan, Whence comest thou? Then Satan answered the Lord, and said, From going to and fro in the earth, and from walking up and down in it" (Job 1:7).* He *"walketh about, seeking whom he may devour" (1 Peter 5:8).* We dare not minimize the potential hazard of this formidable foe. We must recognize Satan's ability to establish his domain in the mind. The Bible calls this a stronghold.

Definition of a Stronghold

A stronghold may be defined as a system of wrong thinking — an established manner of thinking, a compulsion, a set of responses, or uncontrollable habits in a person that are contrary to God's ways. These false systems of reasoning always operate irrationally and unscripturally. Many times the person overcome by sin knows he is doing wrong. Often, he does not want to do it, but he seems to have no choice. He is shackled. The perpetual reinforcement of wrong thinking or wrong action leads to an almost involuntary response. It is similar to a groove on a phonograph record. On each rotation the phonograph needle will fall and play the same tune over and over. Compulsion is the trademark of a stronghold. Forceful, persistent, abnormal urges are symptomatic of strongholds.

The Enemy is so deceitful that we are often unaware of our bondage. We may think, "Well, that is just the way it is." If we operate under false pretenses for a long time, we may think we are normal when we are actually abnormal. During this deception the Holy Spirit comes in to do His illuminating work by making us aware of our need.

Strongholds vary from person to person. Each temperament has areas of special vulnerability. The range of strongholds is as broad as the options for disobedience. Wrong thinking may be reinforced in areas such as lustful thoughts, anger, gossip, eating, jealousy, rebellion, prayerlessness, greed, resentment, insecurity, or rejection. Deeply ingrained sin patterns can be overcome, according to 2 Corinthians 10:4-5: *"(mighty through God to the pulling down of strong holds;) casting down imaginations...and bringing into captivity every thought to the obedience of Christ."*

Note the correlation in this passage between thought, imaginations, and strongholds. The war on the saints largely becomes a battle for the mind.

Development of a Stronghold

Scripture clearly warns, *"Neither give place to the devil" (Eph. 4:27).* To give place is to offer room to operate. We choose whether to yield to Satan or to obey God. Yielding to temptation gives the Enemy an advantage over us.

The whole process begins with a *thought.* Just as the Holy Spirit can bring things to our remembrance, the Evil One also can introduce thoughts to our mind. The power of suggestion is one of the main tools of Satan. This is why Scripture gives us guidelines for proper thinking (2 Cor. 10:5; Phil. 4:6-8).

Once the thought is introduced, the second step is a *consideration.* A consideration is simply two thoughts put together, rehashing the thought that has been introduced to the mind. If not recognized and refused at this stage, it will naturally lead to *desire.* God designed the mind so that thoughts trigger desire. Desire unchecked will produce an *act.* This is where the will takes the impulse from desire and puts it in motion. The act is then committed. Undeterred, the initial act spawns another act and becomes a *habit.* A habit is simply an act repeated. Then the habit, reinforced, develops into a *stronghold.* We must recognize this process in the initial stages and cut it short before a pattern is set.

Chapter 4

Renunciation of the Past

If we are to implement our God-given right to sound thinking, we must recapture our mental beachheads. When we accept ideas from the Evil One, we grant Satan access into our minds. Undealt with, wrong thinking will bear fruit. The reception and ramifications of false notions do not occur without our consent. By yielding to the tempter in an act of will, we give ground to Satan. All sin stems from cooperating with Satan in unbelief and rebellion.

Just as we must make a conscious choice in the development of the beachhead, we must also make a conscious choice to remove false ideas.

"But have renounced the hidden things of dishonesty" (2 Cor. 4:2). Renunciation is breaking every contract, refusing every lie, forsaking all involvement, and rejecting any lingering effect where Satan has been given room to operate. True and lasting repentance encompasses renunciation.

Occult Involvement

"And many that believed came, and confessed, and shewed their deeds. Many of them also which used curious arts brought their books together, and burned them before all men" (Acts 19:18-19). These new believers came and openly turned their backs on these practices. Having renounced this occult involvement with magical arts, they brought their magical books and burned them, in public renunciation of past involvement in the occult.

Many unsuspecting believers dabble in the occult. Others feel no harm can be done *since they do not believe in it.* There is always a hidden price tag with occult involvement. If the actual participant is not affected, quite often his children or family suffers as a result. The word *occult* means "hidden," "mysterious," or "concealed" — forbidden knowledge. Occult practices have accommodated themselves to various cultures, but the underlying principles have remained the same for thousands of years.

God strongly forbids any involvement with evil spirits and occult practices. *"When thou art come into the land which the Lord thy God giveth thee, thou shalt not learn to do after the abominations of those nations. There shall not be found among you any one that maketh his son or his daughter to pass through the fire* [human sacrifices], *or that useth divination* [telling the future], *or an observer of times* [horoscopes and astrology], *or an enchanter* [magic spells], *or a witch* [one who knows], *or a charmer* [removal of warts by charms, removing the pain of a burn by charming], *or a consulter with familiar spirits* [medium], *or wizard* [knowing one], *or a necromancer* [gaining information from the dead, seances]. *For all that do these things are an abomination unto the Lord"* *(Deut. 18:9-12).* These verses seem to comprise the eight original occult practices. Many variations have stemmed from these. God's condemnation of occult involvement was severe. *"Thou shalt not suffer a witch to live"* *(Exod. 22:18).* God made it unmistakably clear that those who follow Him are never to associate with the occult.

Here is a partial listing of occult practices that are popular here in North America:

1. Astrology
2. Amulets — Good luck charms, etc.
3. Astral projection — out-of-body experience
4. Automatic writing
5. Biorhythm
6. Black Magic
7. Calling up spirits — use candles, etc.

    8. Charming — blood, etc.
    9. Clairvoyance
  10. Color Therapy — use lights, threads
  11. Crystal Ball
  12. Divination
  13. Dowsing — form of divination
  14. Drugs
  15. ESP
  16. Fire-walking — pagan cultures
  17. Fortune-telling
  18. Horoscopes
  19. Hypnotism
  20. Levitation
  21. Mind-reading
  22. Necromancy — talking to dead
  23. Occult healing — charming, etc.
  24. Ouija Board
  25. Palm-reading
  26. Ring or needle on thread
  27. Satanism — worshiping Satan
  28. Seances
  29. Sorcery
  30. Table-tapping
  31. Tarot Cards
  32. Tea Leaves
  33. Telepathy
  34. Transcendental meditation
  35. White Magic
  36. Wizardry — using witchcraft to influence
  37. Yoga Cult
  38. Zodiac Signs

Involvement with the occult is only one means of giving place to the Devil. Here are several others:

Anger. *"Be ye angry, and sin not: let not the sun go down upon your wrath: neither give place to the devil" (Eph. 4:26-27).* Disputes must be settled quickly. Do not allow embittered anger to stay for even a day without attempting reconciliation. Failure to deal with it "gives place" or opportunity to Satan.

Unwillingness to forgive. *"To whom ye forgive any thing, I* *forgive also: for if I forgave anything, to whom I forgave it, for your sakes forgave I it in the person* [presence] *of Christ; Lest Satan should get an advantage of us: for we are not ignorant of his devices" (2 Cor. 2:10-11).* Paul knew Satan's strategy of breaking up unity among believers through an unforgiving spirit. The importance of maintaining open relationships cannot be over-stated. Once Satan succeeds in putting brother against brother, the sanctifying influence of the church is diminished. This device is easily seen in our culture, where the fragmented and fractured body of Christ cannot transform its own membership — much less society!

This is one of Satan's most destructive devices. We are responsible for closing gaps, tearing down walls, and building bridges to people from whom we are alienated.

Unconfessed sin. *"If we confess our sins, he is faithful and just to forgive us our sins, and to cleanse us from all unrighteousness" (1 John 1:9).* When we lose sight of the holiness of God we lose sight of the sinfulness of sin. Any area of willful sin grieves the Holy Spirit and allows Satan room to operate in our lives.

Bad attitudes and bad feelings toward others. *"Charity* [love]*...is kind; charity* [love] *envieth not; charity* [love]*...thinketh no evil" (1 Cor. 13:4-5).* God takes our treatment of others personally. *"Inasmuch as ye have done it unto one of the least of these my brethren, ye have done it unto me" (Matt. 25:40).* The reverse is true as well. What is done to other Christians is also done to the Holy Spirit who lives in them. Consequently, all wrong doing toward them is likewise toward Jesus in them!

Attitude is as important as action. Jesus taught that the heart attitude would be judged as severely as action.

We must deal thoroughly with cancerous attitudes and dispositions. Remember, Satan is the Accuser!

Envy, bitterness, strife. *"But if ye have bitter envying and strife in your hearts, glory not, and lie not against the truth. This wisdom descendeth not from above, but is earthly, sensual, devil-*

ish [demonic]. *For where envying and strife is, there is confusion and every evil work" (James 3:14-16).*

The origin of jealousy and strife is demonic. Subtly, satanic forces implant thoughts of comparison and jealousy in the mind. Bitterness soon emerges, followed quickly by strife and all sorts of evil. Jealousy is the only sin from which no one gets any pleasure. Probably everyone has contended with jealousy. Renouncing this sin will go a long way toward bringing our lives under God's control.

Pride. *"Lest being lifted up with pride he fall into the condemnation of the devil" (1 Tim. 3:6).* Paul strongly warned about putting a novice in a place of leadership, lest he be lifted up with pride. Pride was the basis of Satan's fall. Satan's haughty arrogance caused him to wish for independence from God. He was not satisfied to be under God's authority and sought to displace God from His throne. When the "I wills" do not correspond to what "God wills," there is pride. Pride seeks to function independently of God.

Unbelief. *"Whatsoever is not of faith is sin" (Rom. 14:23).* Dependability and faithfulness are not synonymous. "He is the most faithful man in our church" normally means that man is dependable. But faithfulness means full of faith. Dependability is a good quality, "but without faith it is impossible to please him [God]." Doubting and unbelief open the door for the Evil One. Anything apart from faith is sin! The very Son of God did not do many mighty works in one area because of the oppressive atmosphere of unbelief that prevailed. Satan loves cynicism, doubt, pessimism, and unbelief.

Some Christians have given so much ground in this area that they are programmed for failure. Faith releases God to do what He wants to do, and He generally does not act without it. We must replace these unsound thought patterns with correct ones. Unbelief is synonymous with believing a lie. It signifies accepting falsehood as truth.

Genesis gives the account of Joseph's betrayal by his own brothers. Jacob was fond of Joseph and gave him a coat of many colors. His brothers were jealous of him and sold him as a slave to a band of Ishmaelites. They killed a goat, dipped Joseph's multi-colored coat in its blood, brought the garment home, and reported to their father that they had found the coat. The implication was that Joseph had been devoured by a wild beast. Upon hearing the report, Jacob believed a lie and went into mourning. He grieved for years over the loss of his son. He suffered because he accepted falsehood as truth. When we believe a lie, we do not live according to reality. We operate on a false premise. This cripples the spiritual life. Much grieving today is caused by believing a lie. If Satan cannot get us to disbelieve in God, he seeks to have us believe the wrong things about God. Unbelief is simply believing the wrong things.

Rebellion. *"Rebellion is as the sin of witchcraft" (1 Sam. 15:23).* According to this verse, a rebel and a witch are in the same boat. Both are satanic in nature. This verse also states that "stubbornness is as iniquity and idolatry."

"What say I then? that the idol is any thing, or that which is offered in sacrifice to idols is any thing? But I say, that the things which the Gentiles sacrifice, they sacrifice to devils [demons] *and not to God: and I would not that ye should have fellowship with devils" (1 Cor. 10:19-20).* Idolatry is the worship of demons. Not that the idol is anything, but the demon that lies behind the idol is something. Scripture makes it very clear that idolatry is promoted by demons who desire the worship due to God alone. (Lev. 17:7; Deut. 32:17; 2 Chron. 11:15). Stubbornness can be demonic, just as idolatry is. Stubbornness and rebellion give ground to Satan. Paul says we should not be in fellowship or cooperation with devils.

Entertaining suggestions from Satan. At times, Satan communicates directly to the mind. Genesis 3 tells how Satan disguised himself in the serpent and spoke to Eve. *"Hath God said?" (Gen.*

3:1). The serpent served as a mask for Satan, and he has many spokesmen today who speak his thoughts and put his suggestions into our minds. There is sufficient mention of thought implantation in Scripture to indicate that it warrants serious consideration.

At other times satanic forces attack indirectly, causing undesirable feelings such as impatience. If not checked, thoughts of impatience lead to acts of impatience.

Isaiah's prophecy speaks of exchanging the spirit of heaviness for the garment of praise. This is another way of saying, "We do not have to accept this oppressive heaviness, for we can choose to praise instead."

Whether he speaks directly to the mind or indirectly attacks the spirit, Satan seeks to poison our minds with improper thinking.

Evil Companionship. *"Be not deceived: evil communications corrupt good manners" (1 Cor. 15:33).* Evil companionships will corrupt good morals. We tend to become like those with whom we associate. This can be good or bad. *"He that walketh with wise men shall be wise: but a companion of fools shall be destroyed" (Prov. 13:20).* The deceiver seeks to gain an advantage over believers through evil companionships. This is another means by which we give ground to Satan.

Misconceptions of spiritual things. Often, misconceptions of *how* God works aids the enemy. In some circles a misunderstanding of emotions results in counterfeit experiences. Seeking special gifts and dictating to God how He should move paves the way for deception.

Elevating emotions beyond their intended function is an open door for the Evil One. Pride, division, strife, jealousy, and a host of other sins are born out of misconceptions in spiritual matters.

More than Turning Over a New Leaf

Renunciation is more than turning over a new leaf. It is more like burning an old tree! A young lady went forward for counseling. She disclosed she had been associating with old friends and smoking marijuana. She was a young Christian and wanted to repent. This girl did not need to "rededicate" and promise to "do better next time." She needed to repent of the last time. She confessed her sins to God and renounced all past wrongdoing.

Renunciation is a public statement to God and Satan. It is burning all bridges connected with the "old life," forsaking any involvement in non-scriptural practices, and refusing all false premises and ideas that are not of God. A clean break is necessary before any lasting progress can be made in this mental warfare. All ground given to the Enemy must be taken back. If we do not take ground from him, he is likely to take more from us.

Is there a need for renunciation in your life? Are you ready to agree with God and actively turn from all you know to be wrong? Take some time now for serious prayer. Make a list of all the things about which God has spoken to you. Study the following prayer and familiarize yourself with it.

> *Father, in Jesus' name, I confess the sin of (name specific sins and instances). I now renounce it, refuse it, and turn from it. I close every door I have ever opened to the Devil through any occultic practices (name specific area). I now take back any ground I have ever given to the Devil and give it to Jesus. I am a child of God and choose for my life the lordship of Christ. Thank you, Lord, for cleansing me of sin. I am believing You to lead me as my Lord. AMEN!*

Pray out loud a prayer of renunciation similar to the one above. Renounce any ground given to Satan, especially involvement with the occult. Name each area individually. Deal thoroughly as the Lord leads in this area. Do not search your own heart for problems. Allow God to search your heart, and allow Him to show you where renunciation is necessary. Act on this point NOW and join with those who "have renounced the hidden things of dishonesty."

Chapter 5

Reconciliation Where Needed

Satanic forces continually bring up the past. "Look at what you did!" "How could God ever forgive you for what you have done?" Sound familiar? Satan never tells the whole truth, and he seldom tells a complete lie. Quite often there is at least partial truth in his accusations.

Spiritual warfare demands what Paul refers to as *"a conscience void of offence toward God and toward men" (Acts 24:16).* The conscience has a Godward aspect and a manward aspect. There are specific means to clear the conscience in both directions.

A Good Conscience

How is man to obtain a *"good conscience"? (1 Tim. 1:5).* The natural response is that a man has to put things right where things have gone wrong, but is that the way to get a "conscience void of offence toward God"? Some preach, "You will never be right with God until you get right with man." But, if we chase around trying to put things right with so-and-so before putting them right with God, we will probably put them wrong. We cannot get right with God by first getting right with people. We reconcile with people because we are right with God. The order here is the important thing. God first, then man.

The Mind Under the Blood

The only thing that can put a man right with God is the blood of Christ. Modern Christians need to see the power of the blood. *"Having therefore, brethren, boldness to enter into the holiest by*

the blood of Jesus...Let us draw near with a true [tested]
*heart...having our hearts sprinkled from an evil conscience" (Heb.
10:19, 22).* The blood has already been applied from God's side,
but we still need to have "our hearts sprinkled from an evil
conscience." An evil conscience is a violated or offended conscience.

An evil conscience is evidenced by compulsive, plaguing
thoughts of fear, accusation, guilt, jealousy, bitterness, lust, unbelief, criticism, and the like. All the good works we can do will not
free us from a bad conscience.

The Israelites received specific instructions from the Lord for
deliverance during the Passover. They were to kill a lamb and drain
the blood in a basin. Then they were to take hyssop and dip it in the
blood and strike the lintel and the two side posts of the doorway.
The obedient Israelites were to remain inside their homes until the
morning. *"For the Lord will pass through to smite the Egyptians;
and when he seeth the blood upon the lintel, and on the two side
posts, the Lord will pass over the door, and will not suffer the
destroyer to come in unto your houses to smite you" (Exod. 12:23).*
The blood-sprinkled doorway was adequate to keep the destroyer
out.

As for believers, the blood has already been applied from
God's side; but we must appropriate it for our own conscience. The
mind is like a room where visitors are entertained. All thoughts in
our lives come in through the mind, drop into the spirit, and then
possess our whole being. By faith we must see His blood sprinkled
on the doorpost of our minds. When thoughts from the Evil One
come knocking, we simply point to the blood over the doorpost of
our minds. No demon in hell can penetrate the blood! We must take
all our sins and put them beneath the blood.

A Clear Conscience Toward Man

Dealing with God is the first half in reconciliation. We also
need to make restitution on the horizontal plane. Remember,
restitution does not secure forgiveness from God; it results from

that forgiveness. Restitution is doing our part to obtain forgiveness from those we have wronged and doing whatever is necessary to clear the air between ourselves and others. This action is absolutely necessary to maintain a clear conscience. *"Therefore if thou bring thy gift to the altar, and there rememberest that thy brother hath aught against thee; leave there thy gift before the altar, and go thy way; first be reconciled to thy brother, and then come and offer thy gift" (Matt 5:23-24).* God wants reconciliation before gifts, money, or service.

One lady stood in front of her church weeping and said, "I must ask you to forgive me. I am not used to talking to you face-to-face. I normally talk behind your back!" God used this woman's confession of gossip to initiate revival!

A man strapped with guilt was liberated when he went to his employer and confessed to stealing two bags of cookies from the bakery where he worked.

A pastor stood in front of his congregation to ask their forgiveness. "Many of you have been in my office and seen my diploma from seminary. I gave you the impression I earned the degree. I did not earn it. I cheated on my final exam. The diploma has already been sent back to the seminary along with a letter asking their forgiveness. Now I am asking you to forgive me for giving you a false impression about myself."

A 13-year-old girl was bothered about lying to her teacher when she was in the first grade. Victory was her's when she confessed to her teacher and asked forgiveness for that offense committed several years earlier. What a joy it is to have a good conscience toward man.

Our relationship with God affects our relationship with man, and our relationship with man affects our relationship with God. Today little is said about restitution, but the Bible is not silent on this most important subject. Restitution is clearly seen in the action of Jacob toward Esau, and after his conversion, Zacchaeus' desire to make things right was so great that "fourfold" was not too much for him to consider.

Ralph Sutera of Canadian Revival Fellowship has outlined some helpful restitution guidelines:

1. **Restitution must always be a blessing** — never a curse or burden. What God commands you to do will always end in blessing. It should not be attempted until you are certain it will "bless." Timing is so important. Don't rush in recklessly. We are to edify each other.

2. **Restitution results in love.** It should cause more love for each other than you had before. Full joy comes when restitution is proper and complete.

3. **Restitution is a matter of obedience.** Don't sin by disobedience and expect God's blessing. Restitution evidences to man that a transaction has already been made with God. Be committed to making restitution when needed, in God's timing.

4. **Restitution should wait for God to prepare the way.** He provides the circumstances to bring restitution about. In some situations there is no doubt or question about immediate action. In others, God needs to take the initiative. Begin by resting the case with God. Pray, *"Lord, I am personally willing to make restitution and will allow you to take the initiative in preparing the way."* When He does, act accordingly. It is just as important that the Lord prepares the other party to receive you as it is your being willing to go to him. As you are prayerfully "tuned" to Him, God will make it clear. Sometimes the reception may not be to your liking, but when you move in God's way, it will be the way He planned to bring about His results in His timing.

5. **Restitution provides an opportunity to minister.** Often the other party is in need of a "bridge" on which to cross from his self-centeredness into positive obedience to God. Your example and making the move in his direction may free him to honestly face his own need in a way he has desired but has not been able to fulfill. In some cases merely your moving toward him "preaches" a powerful and convicting sermon to his soul, though that is not your

motivation in going.

6. **Restitution is always unilateral** — always one-sided. Never look for the other person to take the blame or even share in the blame. Restitution is specifically a matter of settling my wrongness. It deals only with my blame, my wrongness, in a given matter and must never be related to the possibility that someone else was implicated in my wrong. It is dealing with the attitudes of my own heart that even allow the situation to remain. By understanding my sole responsibility to make restitution, I may move straight to the issue, avoiding the snare of thinking that I must first establish a certain kind of delicate "treaty" with the other party. God's work in another life is His business, though Satan will tempt me to "share" God's responsibility. Therefore, leave the other party with God. Do your part. Be assured that if God asks you to do it, He will not only create the circumstance, but He will also provide the resources needed for you to carry it out.

7. **Restitution is never "IF."** It is never predicated by the statement, "If I have offended you" or "If I have hurt you." The "Please forgive me if I have been an offense" type restitution will never settle anything or produce God's results. If restitution deals with my blame, then it must be that I have offended, hurt, or allowed a bitterness to remain. It then should be "Please forgive me. I am sorry and ask your forgiveness."

8. **Restitution never guarantees or precludes a "Right Response."** At the point you ask forgiveness, you are not responsible or guaranteed a positive "right" response. Commit that to God.

9. **Restitution must always be as broad as the offense but need never be any broader than the offense.** Deal with God alone about private sins of the mind and body. These should never be included in restitution. When the other party knows nothing about it, deal only with God. Never say, "I have had some bad thoughts about you" or "I resented you" or "I have had lustful thoughts toward you and I want you to forgive me." Go to the other party

only when he clearly knows about the situation. If you have shared these thoughts or feelings with a third party, go to him and let him know you have made this right with God. Go no further under any circumstances. Some have "created" thoughts in the other party's mind that were not there previously and "created" a further problem, resulting in continued bitterness and resentment. Private lustful thoughts expressed to the other party can generate these same thoughts in his mind and precipitate a sinful, immoral relationship. Be very careful. Although, with private sins, some people feel strongly that they "must" say something to the person even though it is not necessary and he knows nothing about it. If you are strongly compelled that this is necessary, always be positive, speak in love, edify and make tangible expressions that confirm your love. Never say, "I am sorry for resenting you, please forgive me." Say something like this: "I just want you to know that God has put so much love in my heart for you that I have never loved you more than I do right now. There have been times I should have loved you more, but I thank God for giving me so much love for you now." Follow with tangible acts that confirm your love for him, build him up and bless his life in Christ. Personal sins affecting you and another person must be dealt with at that level alone. Public sins affecting a large group or an entire church need to be made right on whatever level of people they affect. Always be as broad as the offense but not any broader!

10. **Restitution is for the glory of God.** In giving public testimony, restitution brings glory to God only when it exalts what Christ has done rather than magnifying the situation itself. In the light of everything else discussed, personal testimony can be given. It then is not a matter of "hanging out dirty linen in public," but rather an expression of praise to God's glory in deliverance. Others then rejoice by your testimony in that God has performed a miracle rather than in your elaborating all the details. Only when the glory goes to Jesus will people be blessed and the church edified.

IMPORTANT FINAL WORDS...

On matters of personal morality (immorality), be sure to consult your pastor or spiritual advisor before acting in any direction.

Never pressure a person to respond. If he is unwilling to forgive, ask him to contact you when he is ready.

Deal with everything the Holy Spirit reveals.

Aside from matters of personal morality (immorality), the general rule is to deal person-to-person. If impossible, telephone. Letters should be a "last resort."

If you have any questions at all about the what, when, how, or even if restitution should be made, consult your pastor or spiritual advisor.

Do not wish when it is too late you had gotten the right advice. You cannot always recover the damage.

Restitution takes away Satan's ammunition. When things are cleared up, Satan has no legitimate grounds for accusation. God has forgiven you and you have done all in your power to placate the situation. Is there a need for restitution in your life? Disarm Satan by dealing thoroughly in this area.

Related Scriptures: Matthew 5:23-24; 6:12; 18:21; Acts 24:16; 1 Tim. 1:5,19.

Chapter 6

Reckoning on Christ's Authority

"Among the high privileges that spring from the believer's exalted position, seated in the heavenlies in Christ, the highest no doubt has to do with what may be called 'delegated authority.' The believer commands and it is done. In the Name of Jesus the believer exercises 'executive authority' — he commands the mountains to be moved and to be cast into the sea, and if he doubts not in his heart it is done.

It will not do to wave the matter aside and say, but Jesus was not talking about mountains, it is just a figure of speech! He is certainly referring to mountains of a different order. But saying that, we have only augmented the problem. These are the mountains, as all Christian workers know, hardest to move. Science can take care of the former, but who can move the mountains of satanic oppression that are upon the nations and peoples today? Who will remove the mountains of satanic machination interfering with God's Church?"

— E.J. Huegel
The Enthroned Life

The first man, Adam, was created to have dominion. He was given authority over all the creatures in the earth. The beguiling serpent came along and, through subtlety, incited a revolt. At that point the authority given to man was transferred to Satan. Man lost his ruling privilege by default. Satan thus became the "prince of this world." The legal authority delegated by God to man was turned over to Satan.

An Adversary Overthrown

Here is where Calvary comes into play. *"The Son of God was manifested, that he might destroy the works of the devil" (1 John 3:8). "The prince of this world is judged" (John 16:11).* Christ has broken the power of Satan over the fallen race. Contrary to much speculation, God and Satan are not battling it out to see who is going to win. The die is already cast, and Jehovah is the Sovereign Lord of the universe, which in turn means, Satan is a defeated foe!

Satan was the first created being to exhibit a will opposed to God's will. Isaiah 14 records five "I wills."

"I will ascend into heaven."

"I will exalt my throne above the stars of God."

"I will sit also upon the mount."

"I will ascend above the heights of the clouds."

"I will be like the most High."

This self-willed disposition is the essence of rebellion. Satan was the first sinner in the universe. Since that time many have been added to his ranks.

Satan secured man's obedience to his own suggestion and wrested the scepter of authority from man (Adam). Man's allegiance was transferred at that point from God to Satan. Satan gained a victory over Adam, and the whole race plunged into spiritual darkness. Lewis Sperry Chafer comments in his book entitled *Satan:*

> *However victorious Satan may have been over the first Adam, it is certain that he met a complete and final judgment and sentence in the Last Adam, and that the bruising of the serpent's head which was a part of the Adamic covenant was realized. Referring to His cross, Jesus said, 'Now is the judgment of this world; now shall the prince of this world be cast out' (John 12:31). And again in John 16:11, 'Of judgment, because the prince of this*

world is judged.' Still another scriptural testimony to this great defeat of Satan is recorded in Colossians 2:13-15: 'Having forgiven you all trespasses; blotting out the handwriting of ordinances that was against us, which was contrary to us, and took it out of the way, nailing it to the cross; and having spoiled principalities and powers, he made a shew of them openly, triumphing over them in it.' It is clear that, though Satan may have triumphed over the first Adam and thereby became the god and prince of this world, he himself was perfectly and finally triumphed over and judged by the Last Adam on the cross.

In the judicial system a sentence is pronounced and made known before it is actually executed. The criminal is under sentence during this interval, but awaiting its execution. Satan is a defeated foe, but that does not mean he is banished to the lake of fire. The sentence has been decreed, but the full execution of his sentence remains to be carried out.

Why did God leave the Devil in the world? If he is a defeated foe (and he is) why did God not cast him into hell after his defeat at Calvary? One reason Satan is allowed to reign in this world system is that the bride of Christ must be gathered out. The bride of Christ will sit with Him upon His throne (Rev. 3:21; 1 Cor. 6:23; Matt. 19:28). Lewis Sperry Chafer comments, "Another probable reason for the delay in the termination of evil in the world and the execution of judgment upon Satan is that the presence of evil in the world provides the Christian with a ceaseless conflict by which he can alone gain the character of an overcomer." The overcoming of evil forces prepares the believer to rule and reign with Christ. The dethroning of Satan does not mean that he is nonexistent. To the contrary, he and his emissaries provide the divine sandpaper God needs to smooth out the saints!

At the Cross Jesus "spoiled principalities and powers." The

Cross of Christ is our basis of deliverance from satanic powers. The supremacy of Christ is vividly described in Philippians 2:9-10: *"Wherefore God also hath highly exalted him, and given him a name which is above every name: That at the name of Jesus every knee should bow, of things in heaven, and things in earth, and things under the earth."*

"Things in heaven" — sphere of God.

"Things in earth" — sphere of natural realm.

"Things under the earth" — sphere of the satanic realm.

All beings in the created universe are subject to the Lord Jesus Christ. The Resurrection of Jesus dethroned Satan and enthroned believers with Christ!

A Lofty Position

A policeman can command huge trucks to pull off to the side of the road with a mere gesture of his hand. However, you and I can gesture and scream all day, and not even a Volkswagen will pull over! The police officer has the delegated authority to direct traffic. Drivers recognize and respect the power given to the policeman by the state. Without the power that stands behind the uniform and badge he wears, drivers would not respect and obey him. In and of ourselves we are no match for the Evil One. *"Yet Michael the archangel, when contending with the devil he disputed about the body of Moses, durst not bring against him a railing accusation, but said, The Lord rebuke thee" (Jude 9).* Archangels are the highest order of angelic beings. Yet Satan, being of the cherubim class, occupied a higher order than the archangel Michael. Therefore, Michael appealed to the highest power when he said, "The Lord rebuke thee."

Ezekiel 28:12-17 gives us a glimpse of the power of Satan. Prior to his fall, Satan was called the "anointed cherub" — evidently the highest and keenest creature of God's creation. He is referred to as being "full of wisdom," "perfect in beauty," and "perfect in thy ways." Of course this was Satan's biographical sketch before pride entered his heart. The fact that Satan carried a lot of influence was evidenced by his taking a third of all angels with him when he revolted against God.

Though Satan be powerful and brilliant, Christians have no cause to fear. Ephesians gives us insight into the wealth, walk, and warfare of the Christian. One of the greatest needs in the church today is illumination by the Holy Spirit of the believer's present position.

Blessed be the God and Father of our Lord Jesus Christ, who hath blessed us with all spiritual blessings in the heavenly places in Christ:

According as he hath chosen us in him before the foundation of the world, that we should be holy and without blame before him in love:

Having predestinated us unto the adoption of children by Jesus Christ to himself, according to the good pleasure of his will,

To the praise of the glory of his grace, wherein he hath made us accepted in the beloved.

In whom we have redemption through his blood, the forgiveness of sins, according to the riches of his grace;

Wherein he hath abounded toward us in all wisdom and prudence;

Having made known unto us the mystery of his will, according to his good pleasure which he hath purposed in himself:

That in the dispensation of the fulness of times he might gather together in one all things in Christ, both which are in heaven, and which are on earth; even in him:

In whom also we have obtained an inheritance, being predestinated according to the purpose of him who worketh all things after the counsel of his own will:

That we should be to the praise of his glory, who first trusted in Christ.

In whom ye also trusted, after that ye heard the word of truth, the gospel of your salvation: in whom also after that ye believed, ye were sealed with that Holy Spirit of promise,

Which is the earnest of our inheritance until the redemption of the purchased possession, unto the praise of his glory.

Wherefore I also, after I heard of your faith in the Lord Jesus, and love unto all the saints,

Cease not to give thanks for you, making mention of you in my prayers;

That the God of our Lord Jesus Christ, the Father of glory, may give unto you the spirit of wisdom and revelation in the knowledge of him:

The eyes of your understanding being enlightened; that ye may know what is the hope of his calling, and what the riches of the glory of his inheritance in the saints,

And what is the exceeding greatness of his power to us-ward who believe, according to the working of his mighty power,

Which he wrought in Christ, when he raised him from the dead, and set him at his own right hand in the heavenly places,

Far above all principality, and power, and might, and dominion, and every name that is named, not only in this world, but also in that which is to come:

And hath put all things under his feet, and gave him to be the head over all things to the church,

Which is his body, the fulness of him that filleth all in all.

And you hath he quickened, who were dead in trespasses and sins;

Wherein in time past ye walked according to the course of this world, according to the prince of the power of the air, the spirit that now worketh in the children of disobedience:

Among whom also we all had our conversation in times past in the lusts of our flesh, fulfilling the desires of the flesh and of the mind; and were by nature the children of wrath, even as others.

But God, who is rich in mercy, for his great love wherewith he loved us,

Even when we were dead in sins, hath quickened us together with Christ, (by grace ye are saved;)

And hath raised us up together, and made us sit together in heavenly places in Christ Jesus (Eph. 1:3-2:6).

Jesus is seated far above all *"principality," "power," "might,"* and *"dominion."* All authority has been delegated to Him. The Lord and Satan are not presently engaged in a head-to-head conflict to determine who will be victor. The ultimate fate of Satan and all who follow him has already been decided. Satan and demons are presently subject to the authority of Christ.

The above passage in Ephesians tells us Christ is the head of the church and believers are members of His body. The head is where the brain, the control center of the human body, receives messages and sends directions to the hands, feet, and so forth. The various body parts work together in cooperation with the head, not independent from it. Even so Christ, the Head, has chosen to work in conjunction with His body, the church. He does not work apart from us; He works with us. As union between head and members is essential to the human body, so there must be vital union between Christ and the church. "And hath put all things under his feet."

Christ has authority in the spiritual as well as physical realm. This authority, or power, has been delegated to the church to fulfill God's will "on earth as it is in heaven."

Enforcement by Faith

Believers are not victims of the Devil. Christ's victory over Satan is our victory over Satan. The Evil one no longer has any power over the saint who is walking in the light. He may attack, with God's permission, but we are no longer open game to be taken captive by him at his will. *"Because greater is he that is in you, than he that is in the world" (1 John 4:4).* Truly *"we are more than conquerors through him that loved us" (Rom. 8:37).*

Christians have the positional advantage of being seated "together in heavenly places in Christ Jesus." Though the victory has been won judicially, it must be enforced by faith. Many statutes or laws are on the books. However, states and counties must enlist policemen to enforce these laws. They have the power of the state behind them. Likewise, the duty of the church is to enforce the legal defeat of Satan.

Notice the words of our Lord, *"And I say also unto thee, That thou art Peter, and upon this rock I will build my church; and the gates of hell shall not prevail against it. And I will give unto thee the keys of the kingdom of heaven: and whatsoever thou shalt bind on earth shall be bound in heaven: and whatsoever thou shalt loose on earth shall be loosed in heaven" (Matt. 16:18-19).* Also in Matthew 28:18-19, *"Jesus came and spake unto them, saying, All power is given unto me in heaven and in earth. Go ye therefore...."*

Obviously the plan of God is to have the church use its delegated power to execute the bruising of the serpent's head!

Practically speaking, how does victory over Satan become a reality in personal life and practical service? How is the potential translated in the actual? We can do this only when we exercise the spiritual authority Christ has given to us. James O. Fraser wrote:

> *Satan's tactics seem to be as follows. He will*
> *first of all oppose our breaking through to the place*

*of faith, for it is an**authoritative** 'notice to quit.' He does not so much mind formal, rambling prayers, for they do not hurt him much. That is why it is so difficult to attain to a definite faith in God for a definite subject. We often have to strive and wrestle in prayer, before we attain this quiet restful faith. And until we break right through and **join hands with God**, we have not attained to real faith at all. However, once we attain to a **real faith**, all the forces of hell are impotent to annul it....The real battle begins when the prayer of faith is offered. (Quoted by Mrs. F. Howard Taylor, **Behind the Ranges**, London: Lutterworth, 1944, p. 91).*

Satan is not invincible. He is a defeated foe! By faith we are to trust Christ's victory in daily warfare and take our position, "seated with Him." We are with Him because we are in Him. This is our vantage point of victory. We can count on it!

Chapter 7

Resist the Enemy

"Submit yourselves therefore to God. Resist the devil, and he will flee from you" (James 4:7).

The preparation for spiritual battle presupposes submission to God. All attempts to resist Satan will be fruitless apart from total commitment to Christ. Once we meet the condition of submission, we can "Resist the devil, and he will flee."

Putting Satan to Flight

The promise and practice of effectual resistance will excite the heart of the growing saint. The experience of watching Satan retreat in the opposite direction is thrilling, especially after being accustomed to defeat.

We do not have to tolerate a barrage of unholy thoughts, mental assaults, and defeats. We can choose to refuse them by an act of will.

Point to the Blood

"The accuser of our brethren is cast down, which accused them before our God day and night. And they overcame him by the blood of the Lamb, and by the word of their testimony; and they loved not their lives unto the death" (Rev. 12:10-11). These saints used specific means in overcoming their adversary, namely the *blood* of the Lamb and the *word* of their testimony.

Once we are saved by the blood of Christ, we are under God's authority and protection. When our conscience is void of offense toward God and man, Satan has no power over us. Indeed, he and his demonic host are subject to the name (authority) of Christ. In Egypt the blood applied to the doorposts was the means of keeping the destroyer out (Exod. 12:23). By faith we must see the blood applied to the doorpost of our minds. When satanic suggestions come our way we can point to the blood. The blood is the basis of victory.

The Power of the Spoken Word

When Christ was confronted by Satan in the wilderness temptation, He responded by speaking the Word. Note carefully the method our Lord used in resisting temptation.

> *Then was Jesus led up of the Spirit into the wilderness to be tempted of the devil.*
>
> *And when he had fasted forty days and forty nights, he was afterward an hungered.*
>
> *And when the tempter came to him, he said, If thou be the Son of God, command that these stones be made bread.*
>
> *But he answered and said, It is written, Man shall not live by bread alone, but by every word that proceedeth out of the mouth of God.*
>
> *Then the devil taketh him up into the holy city, and setteth him on a pinnacle of the temple,*
>
> *And saith unto him, If thou be the Son of God, cast thyself down: for it is written, He shall give his angels charge concerning thee: and in their hands they shall bear thee up, lest at any time thou dash thy foot against a stone.*
>
> *Jesus said unto him, It is written again, Thou shalt not tempt the Lord thy God.*
>
> *Again, the devil taketh him up into an exceeding high mountain, and sheweth him all the kingdoms of the world, and the glory of them;*
>
> *And saith unto him. All these things will I give thee, if thou wilt fall down and worship me.*

> *Then saith Jesus unto him, Get thee hence,*
> *Satan: for it is written, Thou shalt worship the Lord*
> *thy God, and him only shalt thou serve.*
>
> *Then the devil leaveth him, and, behold, angels*
> *came and ministered unto him (Matt. 4:1-11).*

Jesus verbally rebuked Satan. Each time Satan tempted Christ, He used an appropriate Scripture and addressed the enemy directly.

The spoken word has tremendous power. God spoke the universe into existence. Christ pronounced a curse on the barren fig tree by simply speaking to it. Mountains of satanic oppression can be dislodged by speaking the Word with unfaltering faith. *"If ye have faith, and doubt not, ye shall...say unto this mountain, Be thou removed, and be thou cast into the sea; it shall be done. And all things, whatsoever ye shall ask in prayer, believing, ye shall receive" (Matt. 21:21-22).*

Based on Jude 9, some have suggested that we dare not rebuke Satan. *"Yet Michael the archangel, when contending with the devil he disputed about the body of Moses, durst not bring against him a railing accusation, but said, The Lord rebuke thee."* Michael, the archangel, in effect asked the Lord to rebuke Satan. We must realize that Michael was not "in Christ," but we believers are. God has given to us the distinct advantage of being "seated with Him" because we are "in Him." The angels are curious to look into the mystery of redemption in Christ (1 Peter 1:12). As redeemed saints, we are far richer than we may have imagined. We are equipped by Almighty God that we may be able to resist the Devil and put him to flight! When Satan comes knocking at the doorpost of your mind, point to the blood and speak to the Enemy.

When the unwholesome thoughts come to mind, we must recognize that these are not our thoughts. These are "fiery darts" from the Enemy. Refuse these thoughts and give no place to them. Command Satan and his emissaries to depart in the name of the Lord Jesus Christ. A verbal rebuke and standing on our authority in Christ is our legal basis of victory over Satan.

Chapter 8

Rejoice in Temptation

"My brethren, count it all joy when you fall into divers [various] *temptations" (James 1:2).*

Dread and fear are natural responses to temptation, but the scriptural alternative is to rejoice when all sorts of temptations come our way — to welcome the conflict as an opportunity for growth in character and patience.

Remember the definition of temptation, *an enticement to fulfill a legitimate drive in an illegitimate way.* Being tempted is not a sin. Sin occurs only if we yield to temptation.

A Healthy Alternative

We all have a "personal atmosphere" about us. Those who are sensitive and discerning can often pick up on the vibrations of others. We readily sense despondency, discouragement, or depression in another human being. A person in this state may complain or gripe, or he may not say anything. Nevertheless, his downcast spirit and a total lack of rejoicing is obvious. We are engaged in an unseen conflict, and the Enemy is out to rob us of our joy.

When conflict comes we have choices to make. We can get frustrated and mad: "Oh, no, not again!" We can get worried: "What am I going to do?" We can yield to the temptation and get sad because of guilt, or we can choose to rejoice. Rejoicing is first a choice and then an emotion. *"This is the day which the Lord hath made; we will rejoice" (Ps. 118:24).* Despite our feelings, we can choose to rejoice and praise God. Many earnest seekers have been duped by the Enemy's lie — "You are a hypocrite to thank God when you do not feel it in your heart." Thanksgiving, praise, and rejoicing are attitudes we can choose to exercise despite circumstances. How could Paul and Silas pray and sing praises after severe beatings and imprisonment? They were living above their circumstances and rejoicing, because they saw life from an eternal perspective.

In temptation, rejoicing is the only healthy option. Choosing to rejoice will cause our personal atmosphere to be one of liberty and freedom.

A Positive Command

"Rejoice in the Lord always: and again I say, Rejoice" (Phil. 4:4). Rejoicing is not optional. It is fundamental and foundational. The Bible is saturated with the command to rejoice. There are over 550 references to joy and rejoicing in God's Word. *"Ye shall rejoice in all that ye put your hand unto, ye and your households, wherein the Lord thy God hath blessed thee" (Deut. 12:7).* (See also Deut. 26:11; 1 Chron. 16:10; Ps.5:11; Phil. 3:1; 1 Thess. 5:16). Fulfilling the positive commands are essential in spiritual warfare.

Faith and rejoicing go hand in hand. So do unbelief and complaining. When God delivered the children of Israel from Egypt, He first sent miraculous plagues upon the Egyptians. Then He parted the Red Sea. The Israelites had seen an abundance of supernatural manifestations, yet they persisted in murmuring against Moses. Their complaint was in effect an assault against God. *"Yea, they spake against God...they believed not in God, and trusted not in his salvation" (Ps. 78:19-22).* Murmuring and complaining are the consequence of unbelief. To be found in a state of faithlessness is no small matter. God judged Israel for her lack of gratitude. *"He cast upon them the fierceness of his anger, wrath, and indignation, and trouble, by sending evil angels among them" (Ps. 78:49).* Because of their flagrant unbelief, God sent evil spirits to chastise them! Clearly, lack of rejoicing is a severe matter. Notice the diagram on the following page.

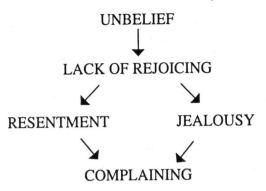

Complaining is characteristic of an ungrateful doubter. Rejoicing is characteristic of a Christian who believes God. Believing God and rejoicing are counterparts in the life of faith. God commands us to rejoice because it encourages and develops a stance of faith while squelching a mentality of defeat!

A Mighty Weapon

Second Chronicles 20 gives the interesting account of King Jehoshaphat and the enemy armies seeking to invade the land. Note the submission and faith demonstrated in Jehoshaphat's prayer, *"Our God, wilt thou not judge them? For we have no might against this great company that cometh against us; neither know we what to do: but our eyes are upon thee" (v. 12).*

God responds to this prayer:

> *Ye shall not need to fight in this battle: set yourselves, stand ye still, and see the salvation of the Lord with you, O Judah and Jerusalem: fear not, nor be dismayed; tomorrow go out against them: for the Lord will be with you.*
>
> *And Jehoshaphat bowed his head with his face to the ground: and all Judah and the inhabitants of Jerusalem fell before the Lord, worshipping the Lord.*
>
> *And the Levites, of the children of the Kohathites, and the children of the Korhites, stood up to praise the Lord God of Israel with a loud voice on high.*

> *And they rose early in the morning, and went forth into the wilderness of Tekoa: and as they went forth, Jehoshaphat stood and said, Hear me, O Judah, and ye inhabitants of Jerusalem; Believe in the Lord your God, so shall ye be established; believe his prophets, so shall ye prosper.*
>
> *And when he had consulted with the people, he appointed singers unto the Lord, and that should praise the beauty of holiness, as they went out before the army, and to say, Praise the Lord; for his mercy endureth for ever.*
>
> *And when they began to sing and to praise, the Lord set ambushments against the children of Ammon, Moab, and mount Seir, which were come against Judah; and they were smitten (2 Chron. 20:17-22).*

Note that "he appointed singers unto the Lord" to lead the way into battle. Who ever heard of sending singers ahead of the troops into combat? Humanly speaking, this is a strange way to wage war. But in the spiritual realm, this is normal procedure. Rejoicing, praise, and thanksgiving are mighty weapons that pave the way to victory against spiritual adversaries.

Satan is said to be allergic to praise. In the Shantung revival, demon-possessed people were ushered into the midst of rejoicing Christians who were singing and praising God. Reportedly, no demon could stand its ground for more than an hour in the midst of praise! Satanic forces thrive where there is unbelief, turmoil, murmuring, and criticizing. However, praise is repulsive to Satan and demons.

"O thou that inhabitest the praises of Israel" (Ps. 22:3). God inhabits praise. As it has been stated, "Praise is God's address." God lives in the midst of praise. The Ark of the Covenant was the receptacle for the Testimony (tablets of stone with God's commandments on them). The mercy seat was a solid gold lid for the

Ark. Two cherubim of gold with outstretched wings were placed on the mercy seat facing each other. The cherubim were symbols of the presence of Jehovah. God prescribed this as His meeting place with Israel, *"And there I will meet with thee, and I will commune with thee from above the mercy seat, from between the two cherubims which are upon the ark of the testimony" (Exod. 25:22).* Frequent reference is made to Jehovah dwelling between the cherubim (Num. 7:89; 1 Sam. 4:4; Ps. 80:1). The golden cherubim on the mercy seat were an earthly symbol of the heavenly reality where an unceasing stream of praise issues to God. Praise and His presence have a natural affinity. Wherever there is adoration and worship of God, He openly manifests His presence. When God who is Light is near, darkness is exposed and repelled. Therefore rejoicing is a powerful weapon in resisting the Enemy.

Prayer and praise play an integral part in implementing God's will.

> *Let the saints be joyful in glory: let them sing aloud upon their beds.*
>
> *Let the high praises of God be in their mouth, and a two-edged sword in their hand;*
>
> *To execute vengeance upon the heathen, and punishments upon the people;*
>
> *To bind their kings with chains, and their nobles with fetters of iron;*
>
> *To execute upon them the judgment written: this honour have all his saints. Praise ye the Lord (Ps. 149:5-9).*

The rejoicing heart, praising lips, and the spoken Word are vital to implementing God's plan. Praise encourages the soul, releases the power of God, and defeats the Enemy!

Chapter 9

Rhythm and the Thought Life

Music is a powerful tool of communication. The style of music as well as the words of the song create definite impressions upon the listener.

Satan was a musician. God created him with musical talent. Most commentators agree that the bizarre description of the King of Tyrus in Ezekiel 28 refers to Satan.

> Son of man, take up a lamentation upon the king of Tyrus, and say unto him, Thus saith the Lord God; Thou sealest up the sum, full of wisdom, and perfect in beauty.
>
> Thou hast been in Eden the garden of God, every precious stone was thy covering, the sardius, topaz, and the diamond, the beryl, the onyx, and the jasper, the sapphire, the emerald, and the carbuncle, and gold: the workmanship of thy **tabrets** and of thy **pipes** was prepared in thee in the day that thou was created.
>
> Thou art the anointed cherub that covereth; and I have set thee so: thou wast upon the holy mountain of God; thou hast walked up and down in the midst of the stones of fire.
>
> Thou wast perfect in thy ways from the day that thou wast created, till iniquity was found in thee.
>
> By the multitude of thy merchandise they have

filled the midst of thee with violence, and thou hast sinned: therefore I will cast thee as profane out of the mountain of God: and I will destroy thee, O covering cherub, from the midst of the stones of fire.

Thine heart was lifted up because of thy beauty, thou hast corrupted thy wisdom by reason of thy brightness: I will cast thee to the ground, I will lay thee before kings, that they may behold thee (Ezek. 28:12-17).

The "tabrets" and "pipes" are understood to be musical instruments. In addition to being an anointed cherub, Satan was a musician. Could Satan have employed his musical gift in gaining the large segment of angels that fell with him? No one knows, but he is obviously gaining a large following of human beings today through the medium of music.

Truly Christian music glorifies God. The unified melody and words communicate truth about the triune God we adore. But we are not the only ones who use music.

Much secular music today centers on lust. Themes of unfaithfulness and divorce are the frequent subject of country-western music. Rock music is much more explicit about promiscuous escapades. Graphic lyrics and provocative background sounds paint concrete mental pictures. Some are recommending a rating system much like the one the movie industry uses. This pornographic music is connected to the sensuous beat often employed by rock groups.

Some music causes you to clap your hands; other music causes you to tap your foot; still other styles of music call for body movement. We do not need to watch the Solid Gold dancers twist and rotate very long to know the music is designed to excite sexual desires.

Other popular music themes are violence, the occult, despair, revolution, the use of illegal drugs, and narcissism. It would be interesting to know the extent to which music has influenced our generation of cultural "burn-outs."

Look at the record jackets and read titles of the songs in local record stores. Many of the "hard rock" groups use occult symbols and words on their cover designs. The sensuous photographs and graphic lyrics are shocking. Equally disturbing is the underlying tone of confusion, hostility, despair, and meaninglessness of the materials.

Some feel that music reflects the basic mind-set of society. The vast amount of financial investment in albums, concerts, and media bears this out. Music not only reflects the attitude of society, but also helps shape it. Music can be a subtle tool for manipulation.

The lifestyles of many performers evidence the fact that Satan is still in the music business. The prevalence of unabashed perversion, alcoholism, drug addiction, irresponsibility, and self centeredness (to name a few) should convince thinking believers of the destructive overtones of the "me" philosophy. Several rock stars have died of drug overdoses. The distortion and destruction advocated by some performers are clearly of a satanic origin.

The Important Place of Music

The Bible clearly shows how good music is intended to glorify God and benefit the saint. *"Speaking to yourselves in psalms and hymns and spiritual songs, singing and making melody in your heart to the Lord" (Eph. 5:19).* This verse comes directly after a command to be filled with the Holy Spirit. The result of being filled with the Spirit is a song in the heart. A singing heart centered on God is especially effective in displacing wrong thoughts.

"I will sing of mercy and judgment: unto thee, O Lord, will I sing" (Ps. 101:1). Singing ministers to the Lord. Preoccupation with God while singing to Him is extremely beneficial. *"A merry heart doeth good like a medicine" (Prov. 17:22).* The joyful person is likely to be healthier than one who worries. King David appointed singers and musicians to minister to the Lord (1 Chron. 16:4-10). The book of Revelation mentions a "new song" sung to

the Lamb in heaven (Rev. 5:9). Music was, is, and will be an important means of grace that glorifies God and benefits man.

Take care in selecting appropriate music. Discard all music with destructive lyrics and music that causes feelings of anxiety, hostility, rebellion, and sensuousness. We are what we think, and the music we listen to plants seed-thoughts in our minds. Select music that ministers to the spirit and magnifies God. There is a lot of good music available. If we are discerning, we can select music that will build up our minds and spirits. Positive replacement in music is a great help.

Chapter 10

Renewing the Mind

"And be not conformed to this world: but be ye transformed by the renewing of your mind" (Rom. 12:2).

The many references in Scripture to terms such as *think, mind, knowledge*, and so on, indicate the priority of proper thinking. As we tear down strongholds, there is a need for a positive replacement. The Holy Spirit guides us into proper thought patterns when we allow Him to renew our minds.

The word *renewing* could be defined as a "renovation" or a "complete change for the better." The renewing process is a gradual conforming of the mental processes to the new spiritual world into which the believer has been introduced. This process is not passive on our part. It is a joint effort between the indwelling Holy Spirit and the faculties of the yielded saint. The Holy Spirit initiates, illumines, enlightens, and quickens the mind. The believer integrates truth by reception, meditation, and obedience.

Believing a Lie

Believers can accept and believe a lie. Jacob mourned for years believing Joseph was dead.

Much grief and suffering is caused today because people believe lies. When we accept a lie as truth our perspective is distorted. We must reject wrong thoughts immediately and not allow them entrance into our minds. We cannot keep the thoughts from floating by, but we can choose to refuse them entrance!

We are What We Think

"As he [a man] *thinketh in his heart, so is he" (Prov. 23:7).*
Gaining a biblical perspective is imperative. The thinking apparatus sets the course for a man's life. The mind is like an incubator
where thoughts develop into decisions. Wrong thinking leads to
wrong decisions. Right thinking produces right choices.

The Bible gives clear directions for mind-renewal. *"Whatsoever things are true...honest...just...pure...lovely...of good report; if
there be any virtue* [admirable], *and if there be any praise, think on
these things" (Phil. 4:8).* Negative thinking is characteristic of
unbelief, which is sin. Devastating effects occur when the mind
dwells on problems instead of praise. Our mental and emotional
dispositions have a direct bearing on our physical well-being.
Happiness is a choice. Choose to meditate on positive things.

It is healthy and helpful to occasionally go into a voluntary
quarantine for prayer. Go three days without *asking* God for a
single thing. Instead, give the time to *thanking.* When prayer is
self-centered instead of God-centered, we can pray ourselves into
despair. If all we do is tell God how bad things are, we can get up
off our knees feeling worse than when we started. Of course, God
does want us to cast our burdens on Him, but we dare not stop there.
We must follow our requests with praise and thanksgiving. An
occasional concentration of thanksgiving refreshes and enhances
a stance of faith rather than an attitude of defeat. Consider spending
the next three days thanking God in order to get a proper perspective. This is one way to *"be renewed in the spirit of your mind"
(Eph. 4:23).*

Day by Day

Believers must receive spiritual nourishment if they are to be
healthy. *"The inward man is renewed day by day" (2 Cor. 4:16).*
What a need there is to get alone with God every day to feed the
inner man. The outer man or physical body needs food, exercise,
and rest. The spiritual man has needs also. Since we are engaged
in spiritual warfare, we must not slight the importance of attaining

and maintaining spiritual stamina through prayer and feasting on the Word in a daily quiet time with God.

The Bible states we, *"have put on the new man, which is renewed in knowledge" (Col 3:10).* True spirituality is vitally connected to the mind. The believer must cooperate with the Holy Spirit in daily renewal. Growth in grace includes an expanding knowledge of God's Word and His ways, both in precept and experience. This is the believer's daily renewal.

Renewal of mind and heart produces a sharp sensitivity to spiritual dangers. Spiritual sharpness aids the believer in recognizing the approach of the Enemy and his wiles.

Chapter 11

Robed for Battle

The beginning chapters in Ephesians speak of the wealth of the believer, whereas chapter 6 speaks of the unseen conflict against spiritual foes. The first three chapters are rich in revealing the believer's present position, while the last three chapters reveal how these truths relate on a practical level. The whole book of Ephesians progressively prepares the reader for the unveiling of the inevitable combat in chapter 6. The revelations in this powerful book indicate that we are not to expect the Christian life to be a picnic, but a battlefield! Note the progression of words in this warfare: "stand," "withstand," and "stand therefore."

> *Finally, my brethren, be strong in the Lord, and in the power of his might.*
>
> *Put on the whole armour of God, that ye may be able to* **stand** *against the wiles of the devil.*
>
> *For we wrestle not against flesh and blood, but against principalities, against powers, against the rulers of the darkness of this world, against spiritual wickedness in high places.*
>
> *Wherefore take unto you the whole armour of God, that ye may be able to* **withstand** *in the evil day, and having done all, to stand.*
>
> **Stand therefore,** *having your loins girt about with truth, and having on the breastplate of righteousness;*

And your feet shod with the preparation of the gospel of peace;

Above all, taking the shield of faith, wherewith ye shall be able to quench all the fiery darts of the wicked.

And take the helmet of salvation, and the sword of the Spirit, which is the word of God:

Praying always with all prayer and supplication in the Spirit, and watching thereunto with all perseverance and supplication for all saints (Eph. 6:10-18).

"Stand"

Verse 11 states, *"Put on* [be clothed in] *the whole armour of God, that ye may be able to* **stand** *against the wiles* [cunning arts] *of the devil."* No thought of retreat is given here! Robed in the full armor of God, we are to *stand* implanted against the scheming onslaughts of the Enemy.

Verse 12 declares that we are not wrestling against human beings but against *"the principalities, the powers, and the sovereigns of this present darkness, the company of evil spirits in the heavens"* (Conybeare). Here is the identity of the real adversary. Verse 11 speaks of the Devil; verse 12 refers to a martialed host of wicked spirits. Who is the real problem, the Devil or a confederation of vile spirits? We can learn a great lesson at this point. Speakers frequently make light of a genuine encounter with Satan, their logic being that Satan is not omnipresent; therefore he cannot be in several places simultaneously. The Bible does not underestimate Satan's ability or power. Scripture clearly indicates that hordes of evil spirits are under his control, networking information under their sinister head. Recall when our Lord was accused of casting out demons by the power of Beelzebub, the prince of demons. What was Christ's reply? *"If Satan cast out Satan, he is divided against himself"* (Matt. 12:26). Jesus spoke as if the alliance between Satan and demons was so close that they were essentially one. Satan and demons are closely aligned. Of course, Satan is the head, but legions of lesser spirits are under his authority. The phrase, "if Satan cast out Satan," means Jesus Christ referred to the evil hosts and Satan as being on the same team. Whether Satan himself or his emissaries assault our minds, they are in a joint conspiracy. Satan is the mastermind behind these forces. Although he is not omnipresent, we may assume that he, through various channels, knows a lot more than we credit him with. We may be sure that when we address Satan we are rebuking evil.

The Weapons of Our Warfare

"The weapons of our warfare...are mighty through God" *(2 Cor. 10:4).* Robed in full armor, the believer is now ready for action. God has given a powerful artillery to use against the Enemy. Knowing about the weapons is essential, but knowledge alone is not enough. We must employ the weapons if they are to benefit us.

Prayer. Note the first thing mentioned after the admonition to "stand" fully armored, *"praying always with all prayer" (Eph. 6:18).* Prayer not only prepares us for battle, it is the battle! Satan knows prayer is a powerful weapon and seeks to keep the saints from praying. *"As we went to prayer, a certain damsel possessed with a spirit of divination met us" (Acts 16:16).* Paul knew all too well that Satan seeks to hinder prayer, because nothing happens in the world apart from prayer. It is the chief means God uses to advance His kingdom in the world. Prayer is not what we do to get ready for the important things — it is the important thing! In prayer we come into experiential union with our Lord.

Satan shoots his thought-darts our way when we seek to pray. He likes to remind us of our *responsibilities, relationships, activities,* and so on. These are good things, but prayer is not the time to daydream about various activities. Another of his favorite tactics is bringing thoughts of *regret,* hurling memories of failure and unhappy experiences into the mind. Various sins of the past loom larger than life as the foe attempts to divert the saint from prayer. Right along the same line is Satan's injection of a sense of *rejection*. He often lies by telling us that "we are not worthy to be forgiven." He tries to make us forget that we are *"accepted in the beloved" (Eph. 1:6)*. The battle is not only in the realm of prayer, but in beginning the exercise itself.

Ephesians 6:18 admonishes us to pray always with all kinds of prayer. Prayer is strategic, the keystone in offensive and defensive maneuvers. Prayer cannot be overestimated in spiritual warfare.

Praise-Thanksgiving-Rejoicing. These three weapons vary in their essence; nevertheless, they are linked together by similarity.

Praise deals with appreciation for the person of God. God loves praise and He inhabits praise. His presence always means victory! Satan despises praise, so it is a tremendous resource in prayer warfare.

Thanking has to do with the benefits we receive from God. *"In every thing give thanks: for this is the will of God" (1 Thes. 5:18)*. Giving thanks directs our minds Godward. Consequently, the thanking saint is mentally predisposed in the right direction.

Rejoicing is first a choice and then an emotion. Praise and thanksgiving lay the groundwork for an attitude of rejoicing. George Mueller said his first order of business each day was to have his "soul happy in the Lord." The liberation of the inner man by these means gets us into the proper frame of mind. These are mighty weapons against the Enemy.

The Name of the Lord Jesus. Using the name of Jesus means the same thing as using the authority of Jesus. The apostles cast out demons and worked miracles through the name of Jesus. Satan recognizes the power of Christ and is subject to Jesus' authority. We pray "in Jesus name" because we have been granted the right to approach God through His Son. Therefore, we can command the evil hosts by using the authority delegated to us in the name of Jesus.

> *He signed my deed in His atoning blood;*
> *He ever lives to make His promise good.*
> *Though all the hosts of hell march in to make a*
> *second claim,*
> *They'll all march out at the mention of His*
> *name*
> *They'll all march out at the mention of His*
> *name — Jesus!*

The Blood of the Lord Jesus. E.M. Bounds clearly shows the power of the blood:

> *Satan cannot stand an exposition of the blood*
> *of Christ. He turns pale at every view of Calvary.*
> *The flowing wounds are the signal of his retreat. A*
> *heart besprinkled with the blood is holy ground, on*
> *which he not only dares not tread, but he dreads*
> *and trembles and cowers in the presence of the*
> *blood-besprinkled warrior.*
>
> *A clear-ringing word of testimony to the power*
> *of that blood he fears more than the attack of a*
> *legion of archangels. It is like the charge of an*
> *irresistible phalanx which bears everything down*
> *before it. It is the blood applied, and testimony to its*
> *application, the martyr witness in life and by tongue*
> *of the power of that blood is more a barrier to Satan*
> *than a wall of fire.*

The basis of victory is the redeeming blood of Christ. The saints mentioned in Revelation 12 overcame "by the blood of the Lamb." The believer must have his mind under the blood. The application of the blood is for protection. "There is power in the blood — wonder-working power."

> *Neither by the blood of goats and calves, but by*
> *his own blood he entered in once into the holy*
> *place, having obtained eternal redemption for us.*
> *How much more shall the blood of Christ, who*

> *through the eternal Spirit offered himself without*
> *spot to God, purge your conscience from dead*
> *works to serve the living God? (Heb. 9:12, 14).*

The Word of testimony. "They overcame...by the word of their testimony." There is fantastic power in the spoken word. We need to speak of how God has worked in our lives in the past. Say aloud, "God has done this in the past, and He will do it again." Confess the mighty works of God, the past victories you have received, and what you expect Him to do. Scripture lays great stress on the confession of the lips, *"consider the Apostle and High Priest of our profession, Christ Jesus" (Heb. 3:1).*

Truth. We have been instructed to take "the sword of the Spirit, which is the Word of God." Jesus quoted Scripture to the Devil when He was tempted in the wilderness. Memorizing the Word and meditating on the meaning are invaluable resources. The victorious saint is thoroughly acquainted with his *Sword.*

"And ye shall know the truth, and the truth shall make you free" (John 8:32). We must integrate truth into our lives if we are to experience its liberating effect. The truth you know sets you free. The believer must know Christ's victory over Satan, his own power to reject false philosophies, how to use the weapons, and so forth.

The Word of God is an offensive as well as defensive weapon. We must wield the authoritative Word skillfully against the foe, not against people! Satan is waging an all-out attack on the integrity of the Bible. He seeks to destroy the credibility of the Bible because its truth reveals how to defeat him!

The only way to stand in these days is by knowing and using our weapons, for they "are mighty through God!"

"Withstand"

After the admonition to stand and the disclosure of the wicked hosts in Ephesians 6:11-12, we are exhorted in verse 13, to take *"the whole armour of God, that ye may be able to withstand in the evil day, and having done all, to stand."* "Withstand" signifies holding one's ground under attack.

Victor Hugo said, "A good general must penetrate the brain of his enemy." A wise military leader will seek to reinforce the probable point of attack. God tells us to anticipate the "wiles" (cunning arts) of the Devil. These wiles, or strategies, are the maneuvers of satanic forces to damage the people of God. We have all heard of well-known servants of God who fell into immorality, even though they had counseled hundreds of couples with similar problems. One of Satan's strategies is to catch us off guard in a so-called secure area. Satan takes great pleasure in defiling the advancing saint.

The Encounter

The battle is more than a mere moral conflict between the conscience on one hand and evil passions on the other. Paul stated clearly in Galatians 5:24, *"They that are Christ's have crucified the flesh* [evil nature] *with the affections and lusts."* When standing on Calvary ground, reckoning the "old man" dead with Christ, the believer stands in a new position of victory over indwelling sin.

Neither is the conflict merely with the evil world system. Again Paul says, *"The world is crucified unto me, and I unto the world" (Gal. 6:14).* The word *crucified* gives the idea of death. Since we were co-crucified with Christ, the world system has no further power over us. Once we learn how to handle the "flesh" and "world," we discover that the war is with Satan himself!

"Take unto you the whole armour of God, that ye may be able to withstand in the evil day." The battle is not a physical one. It is against the wicked spirits of darkness, superhuman foes we cannot see. Our day is evil and as this age nears the end *"evil men . . . shall wax worse and worse" (2 Tim. 3:13).* But no matter the extent and severity of the wickedness, the believer must *"withstand in the evil day."*

Then too, an evil day may dawn upon one of us individually. This "evil day" may be in the form of persecution, severe testing, tragedy, or extreme temptation. Joseph had such a day. His master's wife attempted to seduce him into an act of immorality, but being strong in the Lord, Joseph was able to "withstand." When wicked thoughts bombard our minds like raindrops on rooftops, we are to stand our ground like Christian warriors. The battle is not ours but the Lord's. If we equip ourselves according to divine direction, we will overcome. If the Enemy returns to attack again, we must maintain our position and withstand in the evil day. No attack of the Enemy will be successful as long as we stand in *"the whole armour of God"*!

"Stand Therefore"

Someone said, "If you don't stand for something, you will fall for anything." God has called us to "stand," "withstand," and "stand therefore."

The believer is to stand fully armored as a good soldier of Jesus Christ. Note the brief description of the believer's armor in Ephesians 6:14-15:

> *"Having your loins girt about with truth, and*
> *having on the breastplate of righteousness; and*
> *your feet shod with...the gospel of peace."*

The belt or girdle of truth, buckled around the waist, was used to support the body as well as to hold other pieces of apparel in place. No soldier is ready for combat without it. The girdle is mentioned first and is called the "girdle of truth." Peter writes in 1 Peter 1:13, *"Wherefore gird up the loins of your mind."* Lehman Strauss wrote in his book *Galatians and Ephesians*, "The mind of the Christian must be clear and discerning, unhampered by selfish, sinful thoughts, guarding against error and the making of wrong decisions. The believer's warfare is dangerous and strenuous and will not permit mental sluggishness. We need to have controlled minds girt firmly about with the Scriptures of truth."

The second piece of armor is the breastplate of righteousness which covered the body, front and back, from the neck to the thighs. It offered defensive protection to vital organs, including the heart.

Any standing is based upon the imputed righteousness of Christ to the believer. But our positional righteousness must be translated into practical righteousness. Our walk must be consistent with our position. Both the standing and the state are referred to here.

Sinning saints will never stand; therefore, *"We should live soberly, righteously, and godly, in this present world" (Titus 2:12).* Righteousness is a matter of the heart, not a pious masquerade. We must maintain strict integrity, with hearts purged and minds clear of every unholy thought. Notice the words "having on." God expects us to be honest and upright.

The feet were "shod with the preparation of the gospel of peace" (v. 15). Roman soldiers had spikes in the bottoms of their sandals to help them keep their balance when engaged in combat. A peaceful heart is a heart at rest in God. Readiness to share the Good News is meant for all soldiers. We need to be prepared for war, or witnessing.

In addition to wearing the armor, we must take *"the shield of faith . . . the helmet of salvation...the sword of the Spirit."*

"Above all, take the shield of faith, wherewith ye shall be able to quench all the fiery darts of the wicked." Faith is indispensable in the battle for the mind. It extinguishes the flaming thought-darts of the Evil One! Satan wants to contaminate the child of God. His weapons are "the fiery darts," those burning missiles shot with lightning speed into the mental apparatus. These satanic fiery darts of pride, fear, envy, jealousy, doubt, discouragement, impurity, hate, bitterness, covetousness, and the like are forged in hell. Our defense is the shield of faith.

"For the Lord God is a sun and shield" (Ps. 84:11). A shield is a protective device. Notice that Paul says, *"taking the shield of faith."* Our shield is the sovereign God Himself, and faith is the human responsibility. God is our defense and protection from these flying missiles. Faith here is complete reliance and confidence in the person, purposes, and power of God. We cannot stave

off the avalanche of flaming darts in our own strength. The believer's bulwark is confidence in Almighty God. He is our "armor of righteousness."

The key to victory is faith. We must actively choose to believe God. We must choose to believe we are:

"seated with Him"
"partaker of the divine nature"
"accepted in the beloved"
"more than conquerors"
"able to stand"
"destined to overcome."

We do not have to stay on the treadmill of resolution and defeat. Believe it!

Next we are to take the *"helmet of salvation."* Adequate headgear is essential. We must have a sure knowledge of salvation if we are to be victorious. A thorough understanding of salvation removes all sense of doubt and fear of condemnation. It is indeed like a "helmet" that repels wrong thoughts. When our minds are operating correctly, we can recognize twisted thoughts more easily.

The believer needs to be saved from his own thinking. We can easily drum up our own notions and accept false ideas. God says, *"For my thoughts are not your thoughts" (Isa. 55:8).* The *"helmet of salvation"* is God's way of readjusting our thought-life. Are you saved from sin? Are you saved from your own thoughts? Are you saved from erroneous concepts? *"Take the helmet of salvation!"* It is available, but you must receive it as your own.

Every warrior needs an offensive weapon. *"Take...the sword of the Spirit, which is the word of God."* When wielded skillfully, the *"sword of the Spirit"* will actually cut through the air and break the oppression in the atmosphere. The atmosphere in some church services is "weighted down." Using the Word against the Enemy clears the air of the "weights." We need to take the sword and wield it against oppressive forces around us. In the context of Ephesians 6 the sword is not being used against *"flesh and blood, but against principalities."* As the Lord quickens the Word to our hearts, we must employ it against the Enemy even as our Lord did when He was confronted with temptation and said, *"It is written."*

"Praying always with all prayer and supplication in the Spirit." The armor alone is not sufficient. The armor suits us to go to the battle in prayer. The great necessity of a good soldier is that he stay in touch with his captain. We must maintain vigilance in prayer at all times, for through it we receive a never-ending supply of strength and wisdom. *"Men ought always to pray, and not to faint" (Luke 18:1).* The soldier is to pray constantly, using all kinds of prayer, and he must pray *"in the Spirit."*

Chapter 12

Reigning with Him

Not all thought problems are directly from Satan. Man is a complex being. We cannot attribute every problem to the Devil. If we are to understand the barrage of mental disorders and psychological problems in our society, we must look at the Fall. When man fell by sinning against God, every aspect of life was tainted. Since the Fall of Adam, not one person has been normal. Some are more severely handicapped than others, but all are handicapped to same degree.

Christ's death on the Cross has remedied man's fallen state and provided for substantial healing in this life—and total healing in the next life. The sacrificial death of Christ was sufficient to bring tangible restoration in all areas of life, especially in the thought life. The day we were saved, God began a process of healing in our minds. Power is available to the yielded saint to *"bring every thought captive to the obedience of Christ" (2 Cor. 10:5)*. Total recovery and perfection will be ours in the next life. But right now the Lord is reprogramming us in large measure. Isn't it exciting to know the Lord is conforming us to His image right now?

Dressing Room

This world is a dressing room for eternity. We are in the process of being prepared to rule and reign with Christ. God is grooming us for the throne (Rev. 3:21).

But in the meantime *"they which receive abundance of grace and of the gift of righteousness shall reign in life by one, Jesus*

Christ" (Rom. 5:17). God intends that we "reign in life" — now. Whatever else this may include, it certainly includes peace of mind and release from incorrect thinking. Christ is victorious over sin, Satan, the flesh, and the world. He is securely "seated" at the right hand of the Father. His unlimited resources are ours *"because as he is, so are we in this world" (1 John 4.17).* His victory is ours right now! Old patterns of thinking will fade away as we are daily *"renewed in the spirit"* of our minds (Eph. 4:23). A pure thought-life is our legal right because *"we have the mind of Christ"* (1 Cor. 2:16).

Victory over Satan is ours for the taking, for when we go to battle in the full armor of God, submitting to Him, the Devil will flee from us. He is a defeated foe!

About the Author

Revival ministry is Harold Vaughan's full-time calling and occupation.

A native Virginian, he was born, reared, and educated in Charlotte County, Virginia. Accepting Christ as a teenager, he felt the call to full-time service, and upon graduation from high school in 1975, he entered Bible College to prepare himself to serve God.

As a college student, Harold distinguished himself as a leader and outstanding preacher, winning the Preacher of the Year Award in his senior year.

Directing a college evangelism team, he traveled extensively conducting preaching tours representing the college.

Graduating from LBC in 1979, Harold entered full-time evangelism. His crusade ministry has covered forty-five states and foreign countries.

He is founder, President, and Director of Christ Life Ministries, Inc., author of several books and booklets, and publisher of the widely read *Christ Life Report* newsletter.

In 1986, Harold was honored among the Outstanding Young Men of America.

Married since 1979, Harold and his wife, Deborah, have three sons, Michael, Brandon, and Stephen.

OTHER TITLES FROM
CHRIST LIFE PUBLICATIONS

FORGIVENESS: HOW TO GET ALONG WITH EVERYBODY ALL THE TIME! by Harold Vaughan.

In a world filled with so much hatred and misunderstanding, few subjects are as timely as forgiveness. And yet, few works of biblical accuracy have been written on this important subject. Vaughan and Johnston's book is the best, purest and most practical treatment of the subject I know. Everyone who has been forgiven should read this book to know how and why to forgive.

Woodrow Kroll
General Director, Back To The Bible

THE NATURE OF A GOD-SENT REVIVAL by Duncan Campbell.

Will it be business as usual or the unusual business of revival? This powerful booklet is packed with power from a man who saw spiritual awakening in his ministry. Thousands were converted when God stepped down from Heaven in the Hebrides.

SINNERS IN THE HANDS OF AN ANGRY GOD by Jonathan Edwards.

This is the most famous sermon ever preached. People in the congregation were gripped in terror as Jonathan Edwards delivered this alarming message. Order several copies TODAY for you and friends!

PRINCIPLES OF SPIRITUAL GROWTH by Miles Stanford.

Principles of Spiritual Growth takes you back to the basics of the Christian life-the cross of Christ, faith, purpose, discipleship, and more. This book by Miles J. Stanford will help you build your life on the solid foundation of Jesus Christ.

*Write today and request an up-to-date CLP Product Guide!

ORDER FORM

QUANTITY PRICES for

"LORD, HELP ME NOT TO HAVE THESE EVIL THOUGHTS!"

1-5 Copies $4.99 Each
6-10 Copies $3.99 Each
11-25 Copies $3.00 Each
26-49 Copies $2.75 Each
50 or More Copies $2.25 Each

Quantity		Total
_____	*"LORD, HELP ME NOT TO HAVE THESE EVIL THOUGHTS!"*	$ _____
_____	*FORGIVENESS: HOW TO GET ALONG WITH EVERY-BODY ALL THE TIME! $4.95*	$ _____
_____	*THE NATURE OF A GOD-SENT REVIVAL $1.95*	$ _____
_____	*SINNERS IN THE HANDS OF AN ANGRY GOD 95¢*	$ _____
_____	*PRINCIPLES OF SPIRITUAL GROWTH $4.95*	$ _____
	Postage: $1.00 to $20 — enclose $2.00	$ _____
	$20 or more — enclose 8%	
	(Va. residents add 4-1/2% sales tax)	$ _____
	Total	$ _____

Make checks payable to: CHRIST LIFE PUBLICATIONS.
P.O. Box 399, Vinton, VA 24179

Name _____

Address _____

City and State _____ Zip _____

*Prices subject to change.